NATIONAL GEOGRAPHIC KiDS

ULTIMATE
Explorer
FIELD GUIDE

Night Sky

Howard Schneider

NATIONAL GEOGRAPHIC
WASHINGTON, D.C.

Contents

LEO THE LION

SATELLITES AND SPACECRAFT

MILKY WAY GALAXY

AURORA BOREALIS,
OR NORTHERN LIGHTS

LET'S GO Stargazing!

DURING THE DAY, NATURE IS MOVING ALMOST ALL THE TIME. Trees rustle their leaves as the wind blows, birds fly past, squirrels race up and down trees, and deer wander through parks and urban woodlands. Everything, it seems, is in motion.

But when the sun sets and twilight darkens into night, nature grows quiet. Animals find shelter, birds settle in trees, and the wind often drops away. After nightfall, nature reveals a different side of itself. If the night is clear and free of clouds, the sky overhead shows a much bigger natural scene than anything we find on planet Earth.

Things change in the sky too. But they change slowly because what you see—stars, planets, the moon—all lies far away from Earth.

When you first go outside on a clear night, the lights in the sky will look few and dim. But if you stay outside, your eyes will adjust to the darkness and you will soon see more. And taking a trip far away from city lights will show you a sky so full of stars that you'll remember it all your life.

Just as birds, animals, and trees change as seasons pass, so will the night sky above. When you become familiar with the sky and its patterns, you'll see tonight's stars slowly give way to new ones as weeks go by and seasons shift.

The book in your hands gives an excellent starting guide to the night sky. Read it indoors, see how it is organized, and enjoy the beautiful pictures and sky folklore from ancient times up to now. Then on the next clear night, take your guide outdoors with a flashlight and start your own exploration of the universe.

—*Robert Burnham, University of Arizona*

HOW TO USE This Book

Outdoor fun doesn't have to stop after the sun goes down. Look up into the night sky, and you'll see more wonders than you can count—from the glow of sunset to the blazing lights of a meteor shower to the constellations that glimmer like jewels across the darkness. You can see many of these night sky specialties simply by looking sharply. Others are clearer with binoculars or a telescope. Some you'll see only through special websites noted in this book, which show you images from high-powered telescopes. Explore them all. First, take a few minutes to examine how each entry in this book will guide you on your adventures after dark.

NIGHT SKY ENTRY

EACH ENTRY HAS AN OPENING PHOTOGRAPH THAT SHOWS A FAMILIAR VIEW OF A NIGHT SKY OBJECT.

FEATURES CALLED "BE A SKYWATCHER" (SEE SAMPLE SPREAD ON PAGE 9) GIVE YOU POINTERS FOR IDENTIFYING A STAR, PLANET, OR CONSTELLATION, AND HELP YOU PLAN FOR MAJOR SKY EVENTS, SUCH AS A METEOR SHOWER.

JOKES AND RIDDLES ABOUT THE NIGHT SKY WILL KEEP YOU SMILING.

FIND OUT SURPRISING INFORMATION ABOUT STARS, PLANETS, AND SKY EVENTS FROM EXPERTS WHO KEEP THEIR EYES ON THE NIGHT SKY AND HAPPENINGS ALL YEAR LONG.

THE MOON

DISTANCE FROM EARTH: 238,855 miles (384,400 km)
ORBIT AROUND EARTH: 29.53 days · LENGTH OF DAY: 27.32
Earth days · DIAMETER: 2,159 miles (3,475 km)

Earth's moon is the only natural sky object that humans have visited. Even without binoculars, you can see the Sea of Tranquility, where Apollo astronauts Neil Armstrong and Buzz Aldrin took the first steps in 1969. The moon has many "seas," though they are not full of water. They are large areas where molten rock has oozed out and hardened into a smooth surface. The largest seas have names and can be located using a chart. Comets and meteors bombard the moon, so a lot of its surface is craggy. (Some of the larger dents and hills have also been named and mapped.) As the moon orbits Earth, the same side always faces our planet at night. The far side may not be visible to us, but it's not dark, as some people think. The sun shines there as well.

THE MOON'S HEAVILY MARKED SURFACE DISPLAYS EASY VISUALS FROM EARTH. TO KEEP TRACK OF THE PHASES OF THE MOON CAROUSEL, CHECK OUT STARDATE.ORG/NIGHTSKYWEB.

EXPERT'S CIRCLE

Scientists studying the moon's origins think it formed when a large object struck Earth early in its existence, knocking off enough material to form a whole new object.

BENEATH THE HEADLINE YOU'LL FIND VITAL INFORMATION FOR PLANETS, STARS, AND OTHER OBJECTS, LIKE OUR MOON, OR EVENTS LIKE ECLIPSES. FOR INSTANCE, VITAL INFORMATION FOR THE MOON INCLUDES ITS DISTANCE FROM EARTH, ITS LENGTH OF ORBIT AROUND EARTH, THE LENGTH OF A DAY IN EARTH DAYS, AND ITS DIAMETER.

THE MAIN ENTRY TEXT GIVES YOU A GENERAL DESCRIPTION OF AN OBJECT, INCLUDING WHEN IT WAS "OFFICIALLY" DISCOVERED, HOW IT WAS NAMED, AND WHAT MAKES IT UNIQUE.

EVERY ENTRY HAS A "SPOT THIS" FEATURE THAT SHOWS YOU HOW TO RECOGNIZE A NIGHT SKY OBJECT. SOMETIMES A PHOTOGRAPH SHOWS A CLOSE-UP OF A PLANET OR A STAR AS YOU'D SEE IT THROUGH A HIGH-POWERED TELESCOPE. SOMETIMES ARTWORK SHOWS YOU A SEQUENCE TO HELP YOU UNDERSTAND HOW AN OBJECT SUCH AS A PLANET INTERACTS WITH ANOTHER OBJECT.

SKY CHARTS

Just as there are four seasons of the year, there are four seasons of the sky: Earth's position changes as it circles the sun and this changes our view of the night sky. On pages 66–85 you'll find charts for these sky seasons, and you'll find out when constellations and other star groupings—such as Leo the Lion and the Big Dipper—are easiest to see.

CONSTELLATIONS

Nearly half of this guide shows you how to find star patterns called constellations. You may already be familiar with many of them. In this part of the book you'll learn more about the constellations you know, and you'll discover new ones.

EACH CONSTELLATION FEATURES A DRAWING OF HOW IT WAS FIRST IMAGINED BY SKYWATCHERS. MANY OF THE STAR PATTERNS WERE SEEN AS MYTHICAL CREATURES FROM ANCIENT GREEK OR ROMAN MYTHS.

EVERY CONSTELLATION HAS ITS OWN SKY CHART WITH A CAPTION THAT TELLS YOU WHERE AND WHEN TO LOOK FOR IT AMONG OTHER STARS IN THE SKY. YOU'LL ALSO DISCOVER THE MAIN STARS THAT MAKE UP ITS SHAPE.

FUN AND EASY EXPERIMENTS BRING INFORMATION TO LIFE BY GIVING YOU A CHANCE TO BE HANDS-ON AND SHOWING YOU HOW PLANETS MOVE, HOW STARS EXPLODE, AND MORE

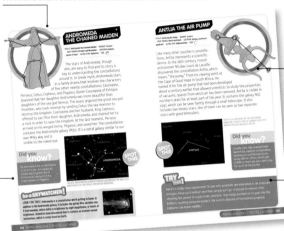

THE "DID YOU KNOW?" FEATURE GIVES YOU A LITTLE-KNOWN FACT ABOUT A CONSTELLATION OR OTHER SKY OBJECT.

SPECTACULAR SKY

Throughout this guide you'll find seven spreads called "Spectacular Sky" that will give you insights into the planet Venus, the yearly Perseid meteor showers, the Andromeda galaxy, and more. A large background photograph will illustrate the topic, and smaller photographs with fact boxes will tell you more about these amazing objects and events in the sky.

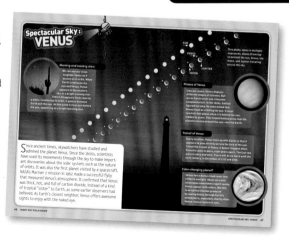

Getting to Know the Night Sky

The moon is one of the most familiar objects in the night sky. It hangs around like Earth's little brother or sister, and everyone on the planet can see it almost every night. But can you find Venus, the planet closest to Earth? If you know where to look, you can view it many nights (and a lot of early mornings) without a telescope or binoculars. How about the Big Dipper—a pattern of seven stars that resembles a giant ladle? It appears most of the time, pointing the way to the North Star. Have you ever seen a "star" that moved? Are you sure it wasn't a satellite in orbit above Earth? You've probably seen a lot of objects in the night sky, even if you didn't know what you were looking at.

Finding Your Way Around the Night Sky

You don't need expensive equipment to be a stargazer. With just your eyes, some help from books like this one, and a little patience, you can learn a lot about the moon, see five planets, and locate major constellations, or groups of stars that form a pattern. And that's just for starters! Of course, it helps to know how the sky "works." When you sit outside and watch it for a while, it seems that the sun, moon, and stars are moving. For centuries that is what people believed. They thought that Earth was positioned at the center of everything, with the stars, planets, and the rest of the universe moving around it. Then, about 500 years ago, the Polish astronomer Nicolaus Copernicus figured out that it all worked the other way around. The spinning Earth travels around the sun. But since we're spinning and traveling with the planet, it seems to us that the sun, moon, and stars are changing positions.

be a SKYWATCHER!

Rule 1: Get outside! Skywatching is an outdoor hobby that you mostly do at night. You can get the best look at the night sky if you and your family find locations with clear views of the sky—away from city lights, if possible. It's also important to dress right. Even warm days can turn chilly at night, so be sure to bring along sweatshirts, jackets, and hats. If it's winter weather, find some thin gloves that will let you take notes or focus equipment. Don't forget water and snacks. Good skywatching takes time.

Rule 2: Bring a notebook and take notes about what you see. There's no need to write a lot. Just record what you observe, as well as the date, time, and any special details. Comparing your notes from different nights will make skywatching more fun over time—and will help you get better at it.

Rule 3: Use a good guide to the night sky, like this one, to plan your skywatching. Check out seasonal sky charts, meteor shower lists, and other information that will help you find objects in the sky. Use astronomy websites to get times and details for what's visible in your local area.

Moon over Saguaro
National Park,
Tucson, Arizona, 2007

TRY THIS!

Why does the sky seem to change when it's really the Earth that's moving? Put yourself in Earth's place: Stand in a room and look straight ahead. Now turn slowly in a circle. Can you see how the view changes and the objects in the room appear to move? The same thing happens as Earth rotates as we stand on it and look out—the stars and sun seem to move overhead.

Ancient Skywatchers

People who lived thousands of years ago kept their eyes on the sky every day.

The sky helped them predict the weather, of course, but it was also their clock and calendar. Though ancient skywatchers didn't know yet that Earth was moving through space in an orbit around the sun, they did notice that the position of the stars and the shape of the moon changed a little bit each day. After centuries of careful watching, they recognized connections between the sky and what happened in the natural world on Earth. They began to understand that they could look to the sky for clues about how to live their lives.

15th-century astronomer

The ancient Egyptians, for example, used the rising and setting of the sun and other stars to position the pyramids and to know when to plant their crops. Many cultures used the moon to measure the passage of time. It takes about one "month" for the part of the moon visible to us on Earth to go from "new" to "full" and back again.

Sailors who lived on the Pacific Ocean islands of Polynesia memorized the positions of stars as a way to navigate across the sea without the help of any instruments.

EXPERT'S CIRCLE

Inca astronomers noticed two bright objects in the sky: One appeared before the sun rose in the morning and the other appeared in the evening after it set. They figured out that they were seeing only one object—the planet Venus. In Inca mythology, Venus became a "servant" that the sun always wanted nearby. At left, a crescent moon lies near Venus after sunset.

Ruins of Machu Picchu

In their isolated city of Machu Picchu in what is now Peru, high in the Andes mountains, the Inca held many sky-related ceremonies. And on hills above their capital city of Cusco, they built pillars positioned to show when the sun rose and set. This helped Inca farmers know when to plant and harvest fields at different heights. The pillars also showed Inca priests when to hold special ceremonies.

Astrolabe: Ancient instrument used to measure star positions

Laugh Out Loud!

What did the thief get for stealing a calendar?

A. 12 months!

TRY THIS!

Sundials were the first tools designed to measure time. They have been used for thousands of years, and it's easy to make your own. On a sunny day, find an open, sunny spot in your yard or a nearby park. Take a long, narrow piece of wood (like a yardstick) and push one end of it into the ground. Notice where its shadow lands? Put a stone or other marker on the ground at the end of it. Wait a bit until the shadow is in a different place. Put down another marker. Repeat this several times. See how the markers are making a curved line like the face of a clock? The curve shows how Earth's rotation causes the sun's position in the sky to change minute by minute.

Tips for Reading the Night Sky

Skywatching is pretty low tech.

The only tools you need to begin are your eyes and your hands. The eye part is easy to understand, but what do you use hands for? Your open hands, fists, and fingers can help you locate objects in the sky and measure them. Distance across the night sky is usually measured in degrees, the way a circle is measured. The whole sky above us measures as half a circle, or 180 degrees. If an object is directly above your head, it is 90 degrees from the horizon, the place where Earth and sky seem to meet. If two objects are on opposite horizons—one in front of you and one behind you, for example—they are 180 degrees apart.

Know Your Degrees!

To make a hand measurement, extend one arm out and spread your fingers as far apart as possible. The distance from the tip of your thumb to the tip of your pinky will cover about 20 degrees of sky. A fist covers about 10 degrees of sky and the length of a thumb covers about 2 degrees. You can use hands to locate and measure star patterns called constellations. For example, if someone tells you that the constellation Orion appears 45 degrees above the horizon, you can spread your hands or stack your fists to help find its location.

be a SKYWATCHER!

LOOK FOR THIS! To locate sky objects, you also need to be able to figure out directions in the sky. Finding north is easy if you have a compass. If you don't have one, the sun gives a clue during the day. It appears in the eastern half of the sky in the morning and in the western half in the afternoon. When you face east, north is to your left and south is to your right. At night, you can get your clue from Polaris, the North Star. To find it, follow a line north from the outer stars of the Big Dipper's ladle. When you stare up at Polaris, you are facing north and south is behind you; west is to your left and east is to your right.

TRY THIS! Practice measuring distance while observing the sun at different times of the day and year. To begin, grab a pencil and a calendar. Then pick a time on a weekend morning and another around lunchtime. Remember to NEVER look directly at the sun (doing so can cause blindness). Instead, look off to the side. At your chosen times, use your hands to measure how many degrees the sun is above the horizon. Record your measurements on the calendar. Check again at the same times in two weeks, then every two weeks for about four months. As the seasons change, the sun will be higher or lower in the sky at the same times of day.

Binoculars, Telescopes, and More

TRY THIS!

Whether you're skywatching at a park near your house or out in the country, bring a flashlight for safety and to read sky charts. But first, you'll want to change up the flashlight a bit. Its white light causes your pupils to get smaller and prevents you from seeing stars as well. Red light, though, lets you see and read without losing your night vision. So go to an art-supply or hardware store and buy red-colored plastic film. Cut out a circle big enough to fit over the end of your flashlight. Hold it in place with tape or a rubber band. You're good to go!

While there are many cool things to see in the sky with just your eyes, binoculars and telescopes let you see moon craters, the rings of Saturn, and even other galaxies.

Binoculars are a side-by-side pair of small telescopes. They gather light and magnify images, typically seven to ten times. A telescope has either a large lens or a mirror that collects light to make an image. You look at the image with a magnifier lens called an eyepiece. When you buy skygazing equipment, it's better to get good quality than worry about the instrument's size or magnifying power.

Many skywatchers get binoculars first and learn their way around the sky before they buy a telescope. Your family may already own a pair of binoculars. Binoculars are listed by numbers such as 7x35, 8x40, or 7x50. The first number is the amount of magnification and the second is the diameter of the light-collecting lens in millimeters. Most people are able to hold 7x or 8x binoculars steady, making it easier to get a good view of the sky. Buying a telescope is a lot more complicated and expensive. There are many different types and sizes. Look for one with a stand that can hold the scope very steady, an eyepiece with a diameter of 1.25 inches (3.18 cm), and an overall size that you'll want to take out and use often.

EXPERT'S CIRCLE

You will see low-priced telescopes in discount stores that promise on the box to let you "See 800x!" Avoid these. They usually have poor optical quality, are difficult to focus, and are shaky on their stands.

The Sky
Above Us!

LOOK FOR THIS! You don't need to look at the sun or moon to know they are there. If you live near the ocean, you can see their presence in another way. The daily cycle of high and low tides is caused mainly by the gravity of the moon (and to a lesser degree the sun) tugging on the water that covers most of Earth's surface. High tides happen twice a day because the moon is always pulling on the side of Earth that it is facing. Tides rise on the opposite side at the same time because the moon is pulling Earth away from the water. When the sun and moon line up and both pull in the same direction, that causes the extra high tide known as a spring tide. When the sun and moon are much farther apart, that makes for a lower neap tide.

It's awesome to think about setting up your telescope in a dark country field and spotting another galaxy, the giant collections of stars that are the building blocks of the universe. But far-off objects like galaxies will appear tiny even through the best telescope. Some of the coolest things to see in the night sky are much closer, look bigger, and can be seen by just walking outside and looking up! Some occur within Earth's own atmosphere, the layer of oxygen and other gases that extends to about 300 miles (480 km) above our planet.

Aurora borealis, or northern lights

Eclipse of the sun

Shows in the Sky

Lunar and solar eclipses are among the best sky shows to watch. They can even help show you the roundness of Earth. (Earth's curved shadow is the big clue.) Satellites, space junk, and the dancing magnetic glow of the northern lights are all also visible to the naked eye. They exist right on the doorstep of outer space. In the pages to come you'll discover lots about sky objects and phenomena in the magnificent sky. You'll also get tips on where and when to get the best views!

NAME GAME

The word "lunatic" comes from "Luna," the Latin name for the moon, and the old belief that the moon caused odd behaviors. It was thought that the moon's phases (changes in its visible shape) each month led some people to act out in strange ways.

TRY THIS!

If the moon and sun are tugging on Earth's oceans, why doesn't the water get pulled into space? The answer is gravity. Just as the moon tugs on Earth, Earth tugs on the moon—and also tugs more strongly on its own oceans. Since Earth is so much larger than the moon, Earth wins that tug of war and the oceans stay on Earth. To see this in action, tie a soft ball or small pillow to the end of a string and spin it quickly (but carefully) over your head. You can feel how the spinning motion makes the object want to fly away. But the strength of your arm and body are more powerful, like Earth's gravitational pull, so it stays put.

It's been a nice, clear day, and it's a time of year that meteor showers take place. You and your family or friends want to plan a starwatching party out in the country or at a local park. But how will you know the skies will be clear when the evening rolls around? It helps to know a little bit about how to read daytime clouds to make a good guess about whether the night is going to be clear. White streaks high in the sky during the day, known as cirrus clouds, are generally a sign of good weather—but they may not fully disappear at night. Puffy cumulus clouds are what you want to see while the sun is out. They will often scatter at sundown or shortly after, leaving the night sky clear for viewing. But if those cumulus clouds begin to stack up, especially in the warmer months, they may build into storm clouds—and then it's better to plan your trip for another evening. You'll always want to go starwatching somewhere that shows as much of the sky as possible, like a field with few trees or the top of an apartment building in the city. But if you stargaze in the city, its bright lights might make some sky objects more difficult to see. Always have family or friends along to share the sights—and for safety!

be a SKYWATCHER!

LOOK FOR THIS! Clouds that appear at a medium or lower height tend to cover more of the sky. During warm weather, they can build into towering thunderheads. These large black masses that give us thunderstorms are known as cumulonimbus clouds. If you see a thunderhead, it is best to get indoors—fast!

SUNRISE AND SUNSET

Sunrise begins the day and sunset ends it. At each time, light from the sun strikes Earth at its sharpest angles. This light comes from farther away than when the sun is directly overhead. Depending on the atmosphere, the type and thickness of the clouds, and your location, the light shines in an array of vibrant colors. Over time, sunrises and sunsets can also show the workings of our solar system. Starting at sunrise early in the morning, the sun appears to travel across the sky in an arc throughout the day. That imaginary line is called the ecliptic, and it mirrors Earth's orbit. (Remember, Earth is rotating and traveling, not the sun.) The point of sunrise, the path of the ecliptic, and the point of sunset change a bit each day. In winter, they are shorter and lower. In summer, they are longer and higher.

Did you know?

Light from the sun travels as waves that have different wavelengths. The longest waves of visible light appear red. Violet light has the shortest waves. It's easy to remember the color spectrum, or range, of visible light with the "name" ROY-G-BIV: red, orange, yellow, green, blue, indigo, violet.

be a SKYWATCHER!

LOOK FOR THIS! As the sun sets, the atmosphere scatters the sunlight. Blue colors scatter first, and then green, yellow, and finally orange when the sun is lowest. This is why a setting sun itself often looks red—all other colors of visible light have already scattered. Sometimes, if the air is very clean and you have a clear view of the horizon, you'll see a surprise as the last bit of sunlight disappears: a quick green flash. The flash makes for an awesome sight over the ocean, from a mountain peak, or out a plane window.

PHASES OF THE MOON

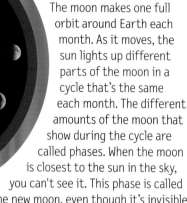

The moon makes one full orbit around Earth each month. As it moves, the sun lights up different parts of the moon in a cycle that's the same each month. The different amounts of the moon that show during the cycle are called phases. When the moon is closest to the sun in the sky, you can't see it. This phase is called the new moon, even though it's invisible to us. A few evenings later, you can see a sliver of the moon lit up in the southwestern sky soon after sundown. That's the crescent moon phase. Each night, the moon's lit-up part grows. When the moon looks half-lit, the phase is called first quarter because the moon has completed the first quarter of its monthly orbit. The full moon comes when the whole face of the moon is sunlit—and very bright! After the full moon (halfway through the cycle), the sunlit part begins to shrink. The last quarter is another half-lit moon face. As the cycle is ending, the moon becomes a thin crescent in the southeastern sky just before sunrise.

TRY THIS!

Go into a room at night with only one bright table lamp turned on. Stand with your right side to the lamp and hold a soccer or basketball in front of you. See how part of the ball is lit and part is shaded? The light is the sun, you are Earth, and the ball is the first-quarter moon.

EXPERT'S CIRCLE

A crescent moon occurs near the beginning and end of the moon's monthly cycle. When the crescent is in the evening sky after sunset, the moon is "waxing" and will get bigger for about two weeks. When the crescent is in the morning sky before sunrise, the moon is "waning" and about to disappear until the cycle begins again.

ECLIPSES: SOLAR AND LUNAR

A few times each year, the sun, Earth, and moon line up in special ways and either the moon or sun is blocked from view for a short time. This spectacle is called an eclipse. A lunar eclipse happens during a full moon if the moon passes directly through Earth's shadow. (At most full moons, it misses the shadow.) An eclipsed moon turns reddish orange in color (right, bottom). In a solar eclipse, the moon passes directly between Earth and the sun. The moon and sun appear to have the same size, so the moon can cover the face of the sun for a few minutes (right, top). There are between two and seven lunar and solar eclipses each year. Lunar eclipses are visible any place on Earth where it is nighttime during the eclipse. Solar eclipses can be seen only from certain places on Earth's surface that change with each eclipse, so astronomers often travel to view solar eclipses. You can get dates and viewing information about solar eclipses from this NASA website: eclipse.gsfc.nasa.gov/eclipse.html.

DANGER!

We can't say it enough:
Don't look at the sun! Even looking at the sun during an eclipse can badly damage your eyes. To view a solar eclipse safely, you need to protect your eyes. (Regular sunglasses DO NOT give protection.) Welder's glasses, special metal-coated glasses, and filters do the job. You can buy these at stores that sell telescope accessories.

TRY THIS!

A cheap and safe way to view a solar eclipse is by using a pinhole projector. With a sharp pencil, poke a small hole through a piece of stiff paper. Keep your back to the sun and hold that piece of paper up. Use your other hand to hold up a second piece of paper directly behind the one with the hole, allowing the sun's light to shine onto it through the hole. You'll see the sun's shape and watch it slowly disappear as the eclipse takes place.

AURORA BOREALIS

You don't feel it, but the sun constantly bombards us with millions of tons of electrically charged particles. Sometimes solar flares (see page 30), or intense solar storms, occur and eject massive amounts of these particles. This sets the stage for what we call the aurora borealis, or the northern lights—a shimmering light show in the sky above Earth's northern lands. The charged solar particles spiral into the atmosphere along lines of magnetic force. They strike atoms of oxygen and nitrogen in Earth's atmosphere, causing them to glow. The northern lights are more commonly seen from far northern places like Alaska and Canada. But when solar storms are particularly intense, the lights can be seen farther south, in places like Oregon and New York. Check out spaceweather.com to see if solar storms are strong enough to produce an aurora. On the southern half of our planet, the aurora australis, or southern lights, appear over Antarctica and other far southern locations. If you don't live in a place where you can see the real thing, check out this NASA photo gallery: nasa.gov/mission_pages/sunearth/aurora-image-gallery.

Did you know?

The solar wind constantly blowing from the sun can actually bend the magnetic field surrounding Earth. During bursts of solar activity, the northern lights seem to brighten and dance.

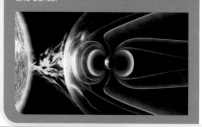

Laugh Out Loud!

Why did the sun do well in school?

A. Because it was so bright!

SATELLITES AND SPACECRAFT

If you watch the sky carefully, you will eventually see a small dot of light cross overhead. It's moving too fast to be a star and too slow to be a meteor, or shooting star. It isn't a plane, either—its flashing red and white lights give it away. So what is it? It's probably one of the hundreds of satellites that orbit Earth and are visible to the naked eye. Satellites collect data and send signals, such as GPS information. They orbit from about 1,000 to more than 35,000 miles (1,600 to 56,000 km) above Earth. Spacecraft orbit, too, and sometimes are visible. The International Space Station (ISS) and the Hubble Space Telescope are among the many craft helping us learn more about the universe. The best time for spotting satellites or spacecraft is just after sunset or before sunrise. That's when the sky is dark, but a satellite traveling high in its orbit is in full sunlight and reflects the maximum amount of light. The ISS is the biggest spacecraft in the sky, orbiting Earth several times a day. According to NASA, a visible satellite passes overhead about every 15 minutes!

EXPERT'S CIRCLE

More than half a million human-made items orbit in space. Apart from working satellites and the International Space Station, many of these items are junk. They include rocket boosters, nonworking satellites, tools dropped by astronauts on space walks—and space station garbage! Space junk can be a danger to functioning spacecraft and satellites and can become Earth junk when it falls from the sky.

TRY THIS!

Check out iss.astroviewer.net to learn when the International Space Station can be seen in your area. Then go out and spot it!

Spectacular Sky: Conjunctions

The moon and its companions

The moon's monthly orbit around Earth gives it chances for conjunctions when it passes bright stars and planets, or a visitor like a comet.

When two or three sky objects appear close to each other, astronomers call that a conjunction, a word that means "joined together." The objects aren't actually joined, though. They just look that way to us because they're lined up in their orbits. From Earth they appear to be in the same sky neighborhood, but they can be millions of miles apart! Chances to view conjunctions may occur 10 to 20 times a year. Most involve nearby planets like Venus and Mars and our moon. These sky objects may line up with a more distant neighbor, like Jupiter, a few times a year. This happens because all the planets orbit nearly on the same plane, or level, around the sun. Websites like astronomy.com or skyandtelescope.com will list the dates and times of conjunctions.

Conjunction of Jupiter, Venus, and Mercury, from top to bottom, as seen from Buenos Aires, Argentina

JUPITER

VENUS

Venus and Jupiter

The two brightest planets occasionally approach each other, and when they do, it is always a cool sight. Sometimes they appear so close they look like a double star.

MERCURY

Triple conjunctions

Once a year or so, neighboring planets like Mars, Venus, and Jupiter will form a triple conjunction. If you start to watch a few days before that happens, you can see one planet outrace and overtake the other.

Our Solar System

SUN

MARS

JUPITER

VENUS   EARTH

MERCURY

Imagine a giant hurricane or pinwheel—but in outer space—a swirling mass of gas, dust, pebbles, and rocks. About 4.6 billion years ago, some of that cosmic mass spun into an ever smaller ball that became our sun. The rest of it remained in the orbit of this sun, forming a solar, or "sun," system of planets, their moons, asteroids (chunks of orbiting rock), and other objects that are held in our sun's orbit. It includes everything out to the strange Oort cloud (see page 44) at the edge of interstellar space. That's an area filled with orbiting chunks of ice that sometimes break free and become comets. The solar system is Earth's home base

EXPERT'S CIRCLE

If you've done any skywatching, you've probably already seen a planet or two and thought they were stars. Venus, for example, hangs around with the moon early in the morning and even goes by the nickname Morning Star. Early astronomers figured out the difference between planets and stars when they noticed that stars seemed to move overhead each night, following a set yearly pattern—and twinkling while they did. The other bright objects that drifted among the stars in odd ways at first seemed kind of unpredictable. The ancient Greeks gave them the name planet, which means "wanderer." They also noticed that the planets don't twinkle.

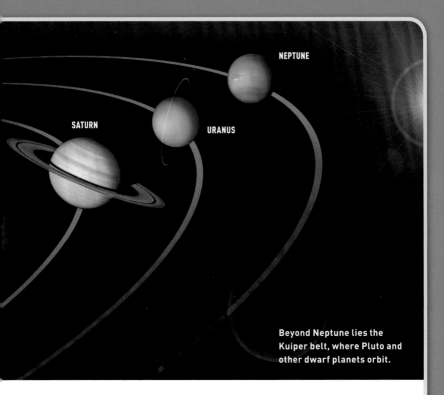

NEPTUNE

SATURN

URANUS

Beyond Neptune lies the Kuiper belt, where Pluto and other dwarf planets orbit.

in the universe, and you can spend hours of skywatching just getting to know the neighborhood. Five of the seven other planets in our solar system can be seen without binoculars or a telescope. If you have a good telescope, you can see the others as well. You can even spot Jupiter's moons and Saturn's rings and locate some of the larger asteroids. It's easy to get started—in fact, you probably already have! When visible, Venus is so bright it is hard to miss. All of these objects orbit around the sun on roughly the same plane, or level, making things a bit easier for newbies to the solar system.

Did you know?

Light-years or astronomical units? Both are special ways of measuring distance that scientists use because the universe is so big. If they used miles or kilometers, they'd have to add so many zeros it would soon get very confusing. An astronomical unit (AU) equals 93 million miles, which is the distance from Earth to the sun. The AU makes it easier to describe how far apart things are in our solar system. Light-years measure much longer distances. A light-year equals the distance that light travels in a year. Light-years are used to measure distances between stars and galaxies. Because light travels faster than anything else—186,000 miles a second (300,000 km/s)—a light-year adds up to 93 trillion, or 93,000,000,000,000, miles (150 trillion km). That's a lot of zeros!

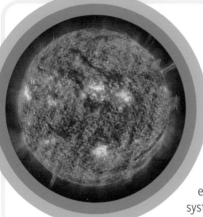

THE SUN

MAGNITUDE -26 · TEMPERATURE 10,000°F (5538°C) · DISTANCE FROM EARTH 93 million miles (150 million km) · TYPE OF STAR Single

The sun is located at the center of our solar system, holding Earth in its orbit and providing the heat and energy needed to support life. There's a lot more to this star than its effect on Earth. It has its own weather systems, for example. Like any star, the sun is a ball of gas. Its center rotates at a different speed than its surface—and faster at the equator, or middle, than at higher latitudes. In a way that astronomers don't really understand, this causes energy to get trapped and build up until it erupts into a solar flare, which is a burst of radiation that can disrupt satellites and other communications equipment here on Earth.

EXPERT'S CIRCLE

Earth's four seasons exist because our planet and the sun are positioned in a way that brings predictable periods of difference in sunlight and temperature throughout the year. Equinoxes mark the start of fall and spring, and are a time when the day and night are about the same length. Solstices mark the start of summer and winter, and are the days of the most (summer) or least (winter) sunlight—days when the sun reaches its highest or lowest point in the sky.

SPOT THIS

THE SUN'S RED, BLAZING SURFACE IS MORE THAN 20 TIMES HOTTER THAN A KITCHEN OVEN. BUT THE STAR'S HEAT CONTINUES TO BUILD IN THE INNER LAYERS, REACHING PERHAPS 27 MILLION DEGREES F (15 MILLION DEGREES C) IN ITS CORE, OR CENTER.

NAME GAME

Many ancient cultures considered the sun to be a god. In Egypt, the sun god was known as Ra. The Greeks called him Helios and believed that the day began when Helios started driving his chariot, pulled by winged horses, across the sky.

MERCURY

RANK OUTWARD FROM THE SUN **1** ▸ DISTANCE FROM THE SUN **29-43 million miles (47-69 million km)** ▸ LENGTH OF YEAR **88 Earth days** ▸ LENGTH OF DAY **58.6 Earth days** ▸ DIAMETER **3,031 miles (4,878 km)**

Speedy Mercury is named after the Roman god whose winged feet helped him move faster than any other god. The planet is speedy because it takes only 88 of our Earth days for Mercury to complete its year, which is a single orbit around the sun. Mercury is also the closest planet to the sun, so it's no surprise that it is pretty hot. The temperature can rise as high as 800°F (426°C) during the day. Mercury is located less than half the distance that occurs between Earth and the sun. This planet can be seen with the naked eye, but only at certain times of the year. Because it orbits so close to the sun, Mercury is lost in the sun's glare for much of the year.

SPOT THIS

TO SEE MERCURY, AVOID THE TIMES OF THE YEAR WHEN THE SUN INTERFERES. LOOK NEAR THE SETTING SUN IN SPRING AND THE RISING SUN IN FALL.

EXPERT'S CIRCLE

An orbit is the path of travel of one sky object around another, as when the moon orbits Earth (left). The travel time of one orbit is the object's year. Rotation is the spinning of an object on its own axis, like a top. One complete rotation is the object's day. Though Mercury's year is much shorter than Earth's because it travels so quickly around the sun, its rotation is slow, taking 58 Earth days to complete one spin.

VENUS

RANK OUTWARD FROM THE SUN 2 • DISTANCE FROM THE SUN 67.2 million miles (108.2 million km) • LENGTH OF YEAR 224.7 Earth days • LENGTH OF DAY 243 Earth days • DIAMETER 7,521 miles (12,103 km)

Neighboring planet Venus is a night sky object that's easy to get to know. It's the brightest object in the sky after the moon, it's easy to find, and it's visible for much of the year. Depending on the time of year, Venus appears at twilight just after sunset or comes into view in the hours before sunrise. Venus is an easy spot for the naked eye, with a steady shining appearance that makes it look like a beautiful star, a quality that may have given it the name of the Roman goddess of love. We see Venus so well because it reflects light from the sun. Its orbit is closer to the sun than Earth's, so part of Venus will be shaded from our view, just like the moon. With a telescope you can see the planet change its phases.

Did you know?

Venus may have a romantic name, but it's not a very welcoming planet. Although farther from the sun than Mercury, Venus has an atmosphere that traps the sun's heat and sends temperatures up to 860°F (460°C). The atmosphere also contains a lot of carbon dioxide and has a thick layer of sulfuric acid. The acid makes Venus reflect sunlight and appear very bright, but it hides the planet's surface.

SPOT THIS

THE ATMOSPHERE OF VENUS MAY HIDE ITS SURFACE (TOP), BUT IT REFLECTS ENOUGH SUNLIGHT TO ALLOW THE PLANET TO HANG BRIGHTLY NEAR OUR MOON (ABOVE).

EARTH

RANK OUTWARD FROM THE SUN 3 · DISTANCE FROM THE SUN 93 million miles (150 million km) · LENGTH OF YEAR 365 Earth days · LENGTH OF DAY 1 Earth day · DIAMETER 7,926 miles (12,755 km)

If space travel becomes more common, more of Earth's residents will be able to view Earth as astronauts do. Astronauts get to view the oceans and continents of our planet with the moon and stars for a background. Sometimes we see the effects of Earth's actions in space, like when Earth blocks the sun's light from reaching the moon, causing a lunar eclipse. Sunlight bouncing off of Earth causes another effect, called earthshine. When the moon is in crescent phase, earthshine often lets us see the outline of the rest of its shape. Earthshine is most intense in April and May for starwatchers in the Northern Hemisphere.

IT'S NOT SURPRISING THAT EARTH WAS NICKNAMED THE "BIG BLUE MARBLE" ONCE IT WAS VIEWED FROM OUTER SPACE (TOP). UP CLOSE, WE SEE THE BLUES AND GREENS OF PLENTIFUL WATER SOURCES AND TREES (ABOVE).

be a SKYWATCHER!

LOOK FOR THIS! Sometimes skywatching means paying attention to Earth's surface. If you're out hiking in the mountains, ask about the location of any dormant volcanoes or hot springs. They show evidence of Earth's superhot, molten center, which was important in our planet's formation.

THE MOON

DISTANCE FROM EARTH 238,855 miles (384,400 km) · **ORBIT AROUND EARTH** 29.53 days · **LENGTH OF DAY** 27.32 Earth days · **DIAMETER** 2,159 miles (3,475 km)

Earth's moon is the only natural sky object that humans have visited. Even without binoculars, you can see the Sea of Tranquility, where Apollo astronauts Neil Armstrong and Buzz Aldrin took the first steps in 1969. The moon has many "seas," though they are not full of water. They are large areas where molten rock has oozed out and hardened into a smooth surface. The largest seas have names and can be located using a chart. Comets and meteors bombard the moon, so a lot of its surface is craggy. (Some of the larger dents and hills have also been named and mapped.) As the moon orbits Earth, the same side always faces our planet at night. The far side may not be visible to us, but it's not dark, as some people think. The sun shines there as well.

SPOT THIS

THE MOON'S HEAVILY MARKED SURFACE (TOP) IS VERY VISIBLE FROM EARTH. TO KEEP TRACK OF THE PHASES OF THE MOON (ABOVE), CHECK OUT STARDATE.ORG/NIGHTSKY/MOON.

EXPERT'S CIRCLE

Scientists studying the moon's origins think it formed when a large object struck Earth early in its existence, knocking off enough material to form a whole new object.

MARS

RANK FROM SUN 4 · **DISTANCE FROM THE SUN** 141 million miles (227 million km) · **LENGTH OF YEAR** 1.88 Earth years · **LENGTH OF DAY** 1.03 Earth days · **DIAMETER** 4,222 miles (6,795 km)

Mars is named for the Roman god of war because of its red color. This dusty red comes from the presence of iron oxide (rust) and other chemicals that cover the surface. Mars shares quite a few similarities with Earth. A Martian day is only a bit longer than an Earth day. Mars also has seasons, an atmosphere, clouds, and polar ice caps. And after many years of exploration and study, space scientists recently discovered the presence of liquid water on Mars. But there's still no evidence of Martian "aliens" or other forms of life on the red planet! Mars shows signs of a lot of volcanic activity, especially around its equator. A telescope will reveal marks from lava flows as well as fields of boulders created from volcanic eruptions.

MARS

SPOT THIS

THE DUSTY REDDISH COLOR OF MARS, SO VISIBLE IN THIS CLOSE-UP (TOP), CAN BE SEEN AS A REDDISH GLOW IN THE SKY FROM THE DESERT IN IRAN (ABOVE).

NAME GAME

Mars has two moons named Phobos and Deimos, the Greek words for "fear" and "panic."

be a SKYWATCHER!

LOOK FOR THIS! Mars is best viewed when it forms a nearly straight line with Earth and the sun. That happens only about every two years. You can find the dates at nakedeyeplanets.com/mars-oppositions.htm.

ASTEROIDS

LOCATION 195 to 307 million miles (314 to 494 million km) from the sun • TOTAL NUMBER: Millions • DIAMETER OF LARGEST: 590 miles (950 km)

There is a gap of 340 million miles (547 million km) between Mars and Jupiter. In that amount of space, you'd expect to find a planet. Instead, it is a zone where millions of asteroids—large and small rock fragments left over from when the solar system formed—orbit the sun in a zone called the asteroid belt. The belt divides the rocky planets like Earth and Mars from the gaseous planets like Jupiter and Saturn. There are not enough rocks in the asteroid belt to make a planet. The total amount is less than the mass of Earth's moon. Scientists have cataloged more than 30,000 asteroids and named more than 12,000 of them. They're supposed to use names from world mythology, but they sometimes name asteroids for friends or celebrities. You can see asteroids through a telescope, but they often look like faint stars. To figure out the difference, it helps to check the same part of the sky hours apart. The "stars" that have moved in that time are usually asteroids!

SPOT THIS

NAME GAME

Each member of the Beatles has an asteroid named for him: John, Paul, George, and Ringo.

THE OBJECTS IN THE ASTEROID BELT VARY A LOT IN SIZE (TOP). SOLAR SYSTEM LEFTOVERS FORM A WIDE BAND OF ORBITING OBJECTS BETWEEN MARS AND JUPITER (ABOVE).

Did you know?

Scientists from NASA keep track of asteroids that approach near Earth, "near" meaning less than about 4.6 million miles (7.4 million km) away. An asteroid strike could cause major damage to our planet.

CERES

DISTANCE FROM SUN 258 million miles (415 million km)
• LENGTH OF YEAR 4.6 Earth years • DIAMETER 590
miles (950 km)

Too small to be a planet but too big to be ignored, Ceres was promoted in 2006 from asteroid to a new category of celestial object: dwarf planet. Ceres is the largest identified object in the asteroid belt. It makes up one-third of all the rock mass there and has a diameter about one-fourth the size of Earth's moon. Like a planet, Ceres is a sphere that orbits the sun. But like Pluto, demoted to dwarf planet in 2006, it isn't big enough to clear the space around it of other asteroids. This means it doesn't have enough gravity to draw other asteroids into itself or fling them farther out into space. Because of this, it doesn't qualify as a "regular" planet.

MOUNTAIN

SPOT THIS

TO VIEW CERES (TOP), YOU'LL NEED TO USE BINOCULARS OR A TELESCOPE. A PHOTO FROM NASA'S DAWN SPACECRAFT SHOWS ITS SURFACE, INCLUDING A FOUR-MILE (6-KM)-HIGH MOUNTAIN (ABOVE). YOU CAN FIND CERES' POSITION AT THESKYLIVE.COM/CERES-TRACKER.

Laugh Out Loud!

How does the solar system hold up its pants?

A. With an asteroid belt!

Did you know?

Some big discoveries in astronomy were made when scientists accidentally found objects while looking for something else. Looking for a planet in the vast area between Mars and Jupiter, Italian astronomer Giuseppe Piazzi found Ceres in 1801.

JUPITER AND ITS MOONS

RANK FROM SUN 5 · **DISTANCE FROM SUN** 483.7 million miles (778.4 million km) · **LENGTH OF YEAR** 11.9 Earth years · **LENGTH OF DAY** 9.9 Earth hours · **DIAMETER** 88,846 miles (142,984 km)

Jupiter is named for the king of the gods in Roman mythology and is by far the king of the planets. It is more than 300 times as large as Earth. It's so big that its gravity controls a sort of mini solar system: the 65 moons that orbit Jupiter. The four largest moons—discovered by Galileo—would count as planets if they orbited the sun. Jupiter is the largest of the gas giants, the group of outer planets that are mainly large swirling balls of gases like hydrogen, helium, methane, and ammonia. And this planet rotates fast, about once every ten hours, constantly stirring up the gases at its surface. But Jupiter takes nearly 12 years to orbit the sun!

be a SKYWATCHER!

LOOK FOR THIS! With binoculars you can see Jupiter's four largest moons: Io, Europa, Ganymede, and Callisto. With a strong telescope you can see the Great Red Spot (above), site of a centuries-long storm on Jupiter's surface that is twice as big as Earth.

SPOT THIS

JUPITER'S ATMOSPHERE HAS FAINT PASTEL-COLORED BANDS (TOP). IT IS THE SECOND BRIGHTEST PLANET IN THE SKY AFTER VENUS. (SEE IT ABOVE AT THE RIGHT, NEAR THE PATCH OF LIGHT.) CHECK OUT SKYANDTELESCOPE.COM/OBSERVING/SKY-AT-A-GLANCE/ FOR ITS LOCATION DURING THE YEAR.

NAME GAME

We know that an alien from Mars would be a Martian, right? What if the alien came from Jupiter? The being would be called a Jovian. Jove is another Roman name for Jupiter.

SATURN

RANK OUTWARD FROM THE SUN 6 · DISTANCE FROM THE
SUN 885.9 million miles (1.4 billion km) · LENGTH OF
YEAR 29.4 Earth years · LENGTH OF DAY 10.7 Earth
hours · DIAMETER 74,898 miles (120,536 km)

If you really like stargazing
and have learned your way
around the night sky with
binoculars, Saturn is a good
reason to upgrade to a telescope. Saturn is the last of the five
planets that are visible to the naked
eye. But to see its famous rings you will
need at least a small telescope. The rings are
made up of rubble, dust, and ice and may also contain the crushed
remains of moons, comets, and asteroids that came too close and were
sucked in by gravity. Every 14 years, Saturn appears to change shape.
Its rings tilt edgewise to Earth, so they can't be seen.

TRY THIS!

To see how perspective
(the way you look at things)
changes your view, hold
a sheet of paper in front
of your face. Now tilt it
and look only at its closest
edge, and notice how
much of the original view
disappears. That's kind of
what happens when the
edges of Saturn's rings face
us on Earth.

SPOT THIS

SATURN

SATURN'S RINGS (TOP) ARE VISIBLE THROUGH A TELESCOPE. THE
PLANET'S SLOW, 29-YEAR ORBIT MEANS IT HANGS AROUND THE SAME
PART OF THE SKY FOR LONG PERIODS OF TIME. ONCE YOU FIND THIS
PLANET, IT WILL BE EASY TO FIND AGAIN. SEE ITS PATH THROUGH THE
SKY AT NAKEDEYEPLANETS.COM/SATURN.HTM.

Did you know?

In the 1600s, the Italian astronomer Galileo reported that Saturn
showed bulges. He actually was looking at the edges of its rings,
as later scientists figured out.

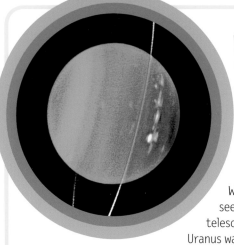

URANUS

RANK FROM SUN **7** · DISTANCE FROM SUN **1.8 billion miles (2.9 billion km)** · LENGTH OF YEAR **84.02 Earth years** · LENGTH OF DAY **17.24 Earth hours** · DIAMETER **31,764 miles (51,119 km)**

Half the size of Saturn and twice as far from Earth, Uranus is too distant and small to be seen clearly with the naked eye. With binoculars it's possible to see its greenish blue tint, and a telescope will show its disklike shape. Uranus wasn't discovered until 1781, when British astronomer William Herschel noticed its brightness and circular orbit during his study of bright stars. Along with Neptune, Uranus is considered an ice giant, with temperatures dipping down to minus 357°F (-216°C). Uranus is a tilted planet, spinning on its side in its orbit, possibly because it had a massive collision with another large sky object.

Laugh Out Loud!

Where does an astronaut park his spacecraft?

A. At a parking meteor!

URANUS

SPOT THIS

URANUS (THE BIG BLUISH DOT ABOVE) IS BEST OBSERVED FROM SEPTEMBER THROUGH NOVEMBER. TRACK ITS POSITION THROUGH THE SKY AT NAKEDEYEPLANETS.COM/URANUS.HTM. UP CLOSE (TOP), IT SHOWS THIN RINGS AND MORE THAN TWO DOZEN MOONS (THE WHITE STREAKS).

EXPERT'S CIRCLE

Scientists can tell a lot about a planet from its color. Different elements give off different shades of light. The blue-green shade of Uranus tells us that methane gas covers its surface.

NEPTUNE

RANK FROM SUN 8 · DISTANCE FROM THE SUN 2.8 billion miles (4.5 billion km) · LENGTH OF YEAR 163.8 Earth years · LENGTH OF DAY 16.11 Earth hours · DIAMETER 30,776 miles (49,529 km)

Neptune is so far out in the solar system that it was "felt" before it was properly identified. In the 1800s, British and French scientists figured out that Uranus's orbit was being affected by the gravity of another planet. This discovery allowed them to predict Neptune's location accurately enough for it to be located. Because of its blue color, the planet was named for the Roman god of the sea and given Neptune's trident, or three-pointed spear, as its symbol. The blue color comes from the methane gas in its outer atmosphere. Closer to its center, though, the planet may actually have large, hot liquid oceans of ammonia, methane, and some water. Exploration by the Voyager 2 spacecraft also found rings and more than a dozen moons.

SPOT THIS

NEPTUNE

USING A SKY MAP AND A TELESCOPE, LOOK FOR A BLUE OR GRAY-GREEN DISK (THE CENTER DOT ABOVE). UP CLOSE (TOP), NEPTUNE APPEARS A MORE CONSISTENT BLUE. YOU CAN FOLLOW ITS PATH THROUGH THE SKY AT NAKEDEYEPLANETS.COM/NEPTUNE.HTM.

be a SKYWATCHER!

LOOK FOR THIS! In the images taken by the spacecraft Voyager 2, you can see a huge stormy spot similar to Jupiter's. This is called Neptune's Great Dark Spot.

Did you know?

Neptune's giant moon, Triton, orbits the planet in the opposite direction that the planet travels. This is known as retrograde motion. If you have a telescope with an aperture of at least eight inches (20 cm), try spotting Triton.

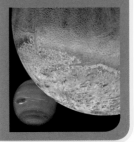

PLUTO

RANK FROM SUN 9 · DISTANCE FROM SUN 3.7 billion miles (5.9 billion km) · LENGTH OF YEAR 248 Earth years · LENGTH OF DAY 6.48 Earth days · DIAMETER 1,430 miles (2,302 km)

Discovered as a planet in 1930, Pluto was named in a contest by an 11-year-old British girl. She sent in the name of the Greek god of the underworld, which also happened to be the name of the popular Disney dog. In 2006, Pluto was demoted to dwarf planet because it did not fit all the new rules for a planet (see Expert's Circle below). Pluto was more like a lot of sky objects scientists recently discovered in the far-out Kuiper belt where Pluto is located. Scientists named these objects plutoids. The New Horizons spacecraft, launched in 2006, finally reached Pluto in 2015 and took the first amazing close-up photos, revealing a distinct heart-shaped marking on its surface (above). It also photographed craters, mountains, valleys, and possibly dunes.

SPOT THIS

FINDING PLUTO MEANS SEVERAL NIGHTS OF SKY-WATCHING WITH AT LEAST AN EIGHT-INCH (20-CM) TELESCOPE TO NOTICE THE MOVEMENTS THAT SET IT APART FROM BACKGROUND STARS. CHECK OUT SPACE .COM/29758-DWARF-PLANET-PLUTO-SKYWATCHING-GUIDE.HTML TO SEE IMAGES TAKEN BY THE NASA SPACECRAFT NEW HORIZONS (ABOVE).

Laugh Out Loud!

Where do planets and stars go to study?

A. To a universe-ity!

EXPERT'S CIRCLE

Scientists decided there were three things that make a planet a planet. A sky object has to have a round shape caused by its own gravity. It has to orbit the sun. And it has to be large enough to clear its path of debris. Pluto, with so many objects floating nearby, failed the third test.

KUIPER BELT

DISTANCE FROM THE SUN 2.5 to 4.5 billion miles (4.5 to 7.4 billion km) • **SIZE** 20 times wider than the asteroid belt between Mars and Jupiter • **OBJECTS:** More than 100,000 objects believed to exist • **DIAMETER** Thousands of objects more than 62 miles (100 km) in diameter

The Kuiper belt is a region of ice and rocky debris that begins just past Neptune and extends through the outer solar system. It is filled with large and small pieces of rock, asteroids, and dwarf planets. Comets often form here too. The Kuiper (rhymes with "wiper") belt also contains the dwarf planets Pluto and Eris, along with Haumea and Makemake, dwarfs named for gods in Hawaiian mythology. Scientists who study this far-out region estimate that there may be hundreds more dwarf planets there, but they haven't found any more "regular" planets. This might be because the Kuiper belt debris is too spread out to have clumped and stuck together to form bigger planets, as the eight planets did during the solar system's planet-forming stage.

NAME GAME

The Kuiper belt is named for 20th-century Dutch astronomer Gerard Kuiper, often called the father of planetary science.

SPOT THIS

Kuiper Belt Object 1998 WW31

Kuiper Belt

Neptune's orbit

Pluto's orbit

Sun

THE EGG-SHAPED DWARF PLANET HAUMEA (ART, TOP) RESIDES IN THE KUIPER BELT (ART, ABOVE). THE BELT BEGINS OUTSIDE NEPTUNE'S ORBIT AND ALSO CONTAINS PLUTO.

TRY THIS!

To see how planets may have formed, fill a big salad bowl about half full of water and crumble some saltine crackers into it. Run your finger clockwise through the water toward the outside of the bowl to get it spinning really fast. Now take your finger out and watch how the crumbs clump together.

COMETS

Each comet has its own orbit and size, but these statistics use the famous Halley's comet as an example: ORBIT AROUND THE SUN **75–76 years** • SIZE OF NUCLEUS **9 miles (14.5 km) long** • DISCOVERED **Predicted in 1705, observed in 1758**

Dirty balls made of frozen gases and dust, comets are leftovers from the formation of the solar system. They begin in the Kuiper belt beyond Neptune or in the Oort cloud, a belt of icy debris that encircles the solar system. Pushed out of their original orbits by gravity, they streak through the inner solar system, traveling in new orbits. When a comet comes near the sun, it warms up and forms a glowing head called the coma. Solar wind makes the glowing tail. Comets that get stuck in orbit around the sun can be predicted to return after a certain number of years and can be seen with the naked eye. To tell a comet from a star, look for the tail and for movement over time.

Did you know?

Comet McNaught, seen here in 2007, is a great comet, one that is super-bright and usually visible for some months.

SPOT THIS

BOTH HALLEY'S COMET (TOP) AND COMET HALE-BOPP (ABOVE) PROVIDED AN AMAZING SKYWATCHING EXPERIENCE FOR THOSE LUCKY ENOUGH TO VIEW THEM. THEY WON'T BE BACK FOR A LONG TIME, BUT A MAJOR COMET ARRIVES IN OUR SKIES ABOUT EVERY FIVE TO TEN YEARS.

EXPERT'S CIRCLE

Two for the price of one! Comets actually have two glowing tails, a bluish one made of ions of gas and a whitish one made of fine dust. Solar wind causes comet gas tails to always point away from the sun.

METEORS

SIZE Varies from a speck of dust to a small asteroid • **PERIOD** Nightly, with annual periods of intense "showers"

You can usually see a meteor if you watch the sky long enough on any clear night. Called shooting stars, meteors begin as meteoroids, pieces of asteroids or bits of debris left behind by comets. Meteoroids streak through space at speeds of up to 160,000 miles an hour (257,495 km/h). They become meteors when they catch fire and burn up as they pass into Earth's atmosphere. If they reach our planet's surface, they are called meteorites. Heavy meteor activity, called showers, happens around the same time every year, and puts on a fantastic show in the night sky. These meteor showers are named for the constellations where they seem to originate. You can find a meteor shower schedule at stardate.org/nightsky/meteors.

SPOT THIS

A METEOR APPEARS AS A LONG STREAK WITH A TAIL (TOP). METEOR SHOWERS, LIKE THE LEONIDS (ABOVE) THAT TAKE PLACE EVERY NOVEMBER, ARE VISIBLE WITH THE NAKED EYE. BINOCULARS SHOW MORE DETAIL.

Did you know?

Up to 10,000 tons (9,000 metric T) of material from meteors—most of it dust—fall on Earth every day.

be a SKYWATCHER!

LOOK FOR THIS! The November 1833 Leonid meteor shower turned into a storm of hundreds of thousands of meteors in a nine-hour period (art, right). Check out the chart on page 153 to plan your meteor viewing.

Spectacular Sky: VENUS

Morning and evening stars

We can see our close neighbor Venus as it passes us in orbit. When Earth is between the sun and Venus, Venus appears in the western sky as a bright evening star. Then it disappears from view for a while. Continuing its orbit, it passes between Earth and the sun. At that point it rises just before the sun, appearing as a bright morning star.

Since ancient times, skywatchers have studied and admired the planet Venus. Since the 1600s, scientists have used its movements through the sky to make important discoveries about the solar system, such as the nature of orbits. It was also the first planet visited by a spacecraft. NASA's Mariner 2 mission in 1962 made a successful flyby that measured Venus's atmosphere. It confirmed that Venus was thick, hot, and full of carbon dioxide, instead of a kind of tropical "sister" to Earth, as some earlier observers had believed. As Earth's closest neighbor, Venus offers awesome sights to enjoy with the naked eye.

SUN →

VENUS →

↑ JUPITER

↑ MOON

This photo, taken in multiple exposures, shows (from top to bottom) the sun, Venus, the moon, and Jupiter traveling across the sky.

Phases of Venus

Like our moon, Venus displays different stages of fullness. But we on Earth never see it become completely full. In the 1600s, Galileo figured out why. He determined that Venus must be orbiting the sun. It must reach its full phase when it is behind the sun, hidden by glare. This helped Galileo prove that the planets revolve around the sun—not the Earth.

Transit of Venus

Every so often, Venus lines up with Earth so that it appears to pass directly across the face of the sun. Called the transit of Venus, it doesn't happen often. Transits come in pairs, eight years apart. The last two were in 2004 and 2012. There will be no more until the next century, in December of 2117 and 2125.

Color-changing planet?

Venus has a dense cloud cover that reflects sunlight. Observers with telescopes sometimes report seeing Venus appear with colors. But this is an optical illusion produced by seeing Venus through Earth's atmosphere, especially shortly after Venus rises or before it sets.

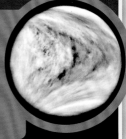

Our Galaxy: The Milky Way

be a SKYWATCHER!

LOOK FOR THIS! In North America, the best view of the Milky Way will be to the south in summer. Because of light pollution, the best location is a remote area on a moonless night. If you look toward the constellation Sagittarius (see page 98), you will be looking in toward the center of our galaxy.

Centuries ago, before most of us lived in well-lit cities and towns, nightfall in summer would reveal a spectacular whitish band running across the night sky. Cultures around the world made up different legends about it. To Native Americans it was spilled kernels from a bag of corn stolen by a mythical dog. To the Greeks it was milk spilled by the mother of the mythological hero Hercules. Today, we know this spectacular band is Earth's home galaxy—the Milky Way. A galaxy is a large collection of stars held together by gravity. In the Milky Way's case, the gravity probably comes from a black hole (see page 61). The Milky Way galaxy has a spiral shape that is home to perhaps 200 billion stars. It is one of the older galaxies known, possibly around 13 billion years old. This is almost as old as the universe itself.

On the Inside, Looking In

Our solar system is located about 25,000 light-years from the center of the Milky Way in one of its spiral arms (opposite). So we're traveling on a planet in a solar system that is in the Milky Way, but we can also view the Milky Way in our night sky. How is this possible? Because of how Earth is tilted, we are looking at the edge of the Milky Way. In the summer, we can look into our galaxy's center to see its densest collection of stars. In winter, we can look at its outer regions. There are many other galaxies in the universe. Galaxies sometimes merge, with a larger galaxy gobbling up a smaller one.

Did you know?

One explanation scientists give about the shape of spiral galaxies like the Milky Way is that waves of pressure sweep around them, kind of like water sloshing in a bathtub. The waves trigger the formation of bright new stars in the galaxy's rotating spiral arms.

TRY THIS!

How far is a light-year? You do the math! A light-year is the distance that light travels in one year. Light travels at 186,000 miles (300,000 km) per second. Multiply the number of seconds in one year by the number of miles (or km) that light travels in one second, and you'll have the answer: about 5.88 trillion miles (9.5 trillion km). Now try this: One galaxy in the constellation Cetus the Sea Monster is 45 million light-years away from us. What would be the length of that trip?

A: 264.6 trillion miles (425.8 trillion km)

Stars in Our Galaxy

Milky Way galaxy

If you look under your bed, you might find a dust bunny, a ball of bits of dust, debris—and maybe pet fur—that have stuck together. That's a start for understanding how stars form. Though the vast space of the universe seems mostly empty, there are plenty of hydrogen and helium atoms, dust, and other matter floating around. Sometimes these atoms of basic matter clump together—like a dust bunny.

The Birth of a Star

If the clump gets large enough, gravity starts to pull in more matter and squeeze it all together in a tight ball. If the ball gets tight enough and the gravity strong enough, the atoms of hydrogen will mash together and give off light and heat in a process called nuclear fusion. Then boom! A star is born.

Did you know?

Our solar system contains one star, the sun. But there may be 100 billion other stars in our galaxy, the Milky Way, and 200 billion other galaxies in the universe.

be a SKYWATCHER!

LOOK FOR THIS!
Many stars are located in constellations or asterisms— two different kinds of star patterns. This photo shows an asterism called the Winter Circle, with the bright star Sirius at bottom center, near the horizon.

SIRIUS

Classifying Stars

Stars are classified by size or mass, temperature, color, and magnitude or brightness (see page 136). There are seven main classes, with letter labels: O, B, A, F, G, K, and M. Massive blue giants, labeled O stars, are the hottest, brightest, and bluest, and may burn out in a million years or so. Smaller, cooler K stars with colors like yellow and orange burn their fuel

at a slower pace and live longer than larger, fuel-guzzling hot stars. Red dwarfs, labeled M stars, are the most common smaller stars and may have life spans of tens of billions of years. Our sun, a G star, was formed with enough fuel to last about 11 billion years. (Don't worry, it still has 5 billion to go!) As a star ages, it goes through stages. First it expands into a giant, then it collapses back into a dying ember called a white dwarf. Many stars travel with one or more star buddies. In this binary star system, two stars pivot, or turn around, a common gravitational point. In a multiple-star system, several stars pivot around the same gravitational point. In the 1700s, French astronomer Charles Messier cataloged many stars and other objects in the sky. Each object name is a number starting with the letter M, such as the star cluster M79 in the Milky Way (see page 62).

TRY THIS!

If there's a gas stove in your kitchen at home, check it out the next time dinner is cooking— with adult supervision, of course! Notice that the flame on a burner is blue. Then ask an adult to light a match away from the stove. Notice that the flame is orange or yellow. Which flame do you think is hotter? Hint: Read about star colors, above.

MIZAR

ALCOR

EXPERT'S CIRCLE

Binary stars are pairs of stars connected by gravity. Other pairs of stars might appear to be connected, but that connection is an optical illusion. These are called optical binary stars. They're too far apart to be connected by gravity. Mizar and Alcor (left) appear connected in the handle of the Big Dipper—but they're actually three light-years apart (see page 49 to figure out how far that is). You can see them with your eyes, but binoculars will give you a better view.

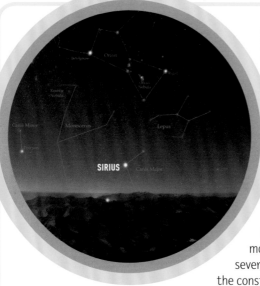

SIRIUS

CLASS A • MAGNITUDE -1.46
TEMPERATURE 18,000°F (10,000°C)
DISTANCE FROM EARTH 8.6 light-years
TYPE Double star

The name Sirius comes from a Greek word that means "scorching." It's a great name for a star that—from Earth—is the brightest object in the night sky after the moon and planets. Sirius has several nicknames. It is part of the constellation Canis Major (see page 113), the Larger Dog, so it is sometimes called the Dog Star. Ancient Egyptians called it the Nile Star because it appeared in the eastern sky around the time of the annual flooding of the Nile River that watered the region's farmland. People have been watching Sirius for a long time, but realized only in 1862 it was part of a double star system. Sirius B is almost as big as our sun, but it is a white dwarf star and is thousands of times dimmer than Sirius A. This makes it difficult to see and study Sirius B.

SPOT THIS

WINTER IS THE BEST TIME TO FIND SIRIUS. FACING SOUTH, LOOK DOWN FROM THE THREE STARS OF ORION'S BELT TO THE LEFT (EAST). LEARN MORE AT EARTHSKY.ORG/BRIGHTEST-STARS/SIRIUS-THE-BRIGHTEST-STAR.

NAME GAME

Attention, Harry Potter fans! In case you didn't know, the character Sirius Black is named for the Dog Star. (And he had a brother named for another star, Regulus.) In the books, Sirius is an animagus, a wizard who can morph into an animal form. In his case, it's a big black dog.

EXPERT'S CIRCLE

Bright stars like Sirius sometimes shimmer, but that's not a quality of the stars themselves. It's the way we see them. As starlight travels toward our eyes, it is bent and shaped by Earth's atmosphere. The lower a star is in the sky, the more atmosphere it travels through and the more it may shimmer. (The "points" on Sirius at left were made by the camera.)

ARCTURUS

CLASS K – Red giant ∙ MAGNITUDE -.04
∙ TEMPERATURE 7200°F (4000°C)
∙ DISTANCE FROM EARTH 37 light-years
∙ TYPE Single

Arcturus is a bright star in the final stages of its life. It has run out of hydrogen for fuel and is now using helium to create its energy. That is causing it to expand, and will eventually lead to its extinction. But in the meantime, Arcturus will stay a featured part of the night sky, the brightest star in the constellation Boötes (see page 110). Spring is the best season to view the Bear Guard star, given that name because it shines near Ursa Major and Ursa Minor, the Great and Small Bears. But Arcturus is moving away from Earth, traveling in a different direction than the stars in its part of the galaxy, possibly on a different kind of orbit. In a million years or so, it may no longer be visible to the naked eye.

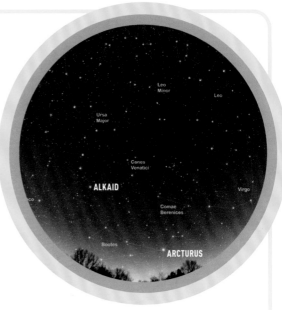

SPOT THIS

TO FIND ARCTURUS IN SPRING, EXTEND A CURVED LINE SOUTHEAST FROM ALKAID, THE STAR AT THE END OF THE BIG DIPPER'S HANDLE, TO THE BRIGHTEST STAR IN BOÖTES.

Did you know?

Arcturus and other old stars are in the "Arcturus stream." They travel together and may have been in a different galaxy that was absorbed into the Milky Way during a collision like this.

TRY THIS!

Craft stores sell packs of glow-in-the-dark stars that you can stick on things. Use them to create constellations on poster board. Start with the patterns of the Big Dipper, the constellation Boötes with Arcturus, and other nearby constellations.

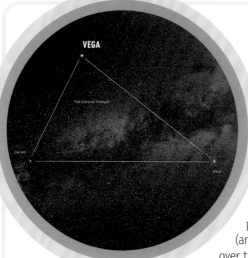

VEGA

VEGA

CLASS A · MAGNITUDE .03 · TEMPERATURE 17,000°F
(9500°C) · DISTANCE FROM EARTH 25 light-years
· TYPE Single

For the earliest humans, Vega, and not Polaris, would have been the North Star—and it will be again in about 10,000 years. Earth actually wobbles as it spins, so the position of north on the sky (and of the North Star) changes over time. Vega is an easy star to find, especially in summer, because all you have to do is look up and find a triangle. Vega, along with partners Deneb and Altair, form a star pattern called the Summer Triangle. This pattern is called an asterism. Asterisms are smaller than constellations and are sometimes part of constellations, but they form distinctive shapes of their own. Vega is also the main star in the constellation Lyra the Lyre (see page 136). Its name comes from an Arabic word that means "swooping." Arab astronomers named many of the stars, and regarded Vega's constellation as a swooping vulture or eagle instead of a harp-like musical instrument.

SPOT THIS

LATE IN THE EVENING IN MID AND LATE SUMMER, VEGA IS ALMOST DIRECTLY OVERHEAD THROUGHOUT MUCH OF NORTH AMERICA.

Did you know?

In recent years, astronomers discovered that the area around Vega is similar to our solar system, with an asteroid belt that may produce planets. This has led them to focus on Vega in their search for extraterrestrial life.

be a SKYWATCHER!

LOOK FOR THIS! If you are looking at Vega in the sky, see if you can find the nearby Epsilon Lyrae. It is one of the few binary, or double, stars visible with binoculars. But there's more! Epsilon Lyrae is actually a double-double star. While you may see it as a single point of light, there are really four stars in the Epsilon Lyrae system. One pair circles around the other pair, held in orbit by gravity.

CAPELLA

CLASS G · MAGNITUDE .08
· TEMPERATURE 8900°F (4900°C)
· DISTANCE FROM EARTH 42 light-years
· TYPE Multiple

Capella is one of
the great deals in
skywatching: It
offers four stars in
one. Located in the
constellation Auriga
the Charioteer (see
page 109), Capella
actually combines the
light of two binary star
pairs. The first pair is two aging
stars that are already running out
of fuel and expanding as they slowly
turn into red giants. Two red dwarf
stars form the second binary pair
in the system. Capella emits x-rays,
but you won't be able to see them.
Scientists have been trying to
figure out the source of the rays
for decades. They think the rays
may be connected to a superhot
cloud of gas that forms a
shimmering envelope around
the star.

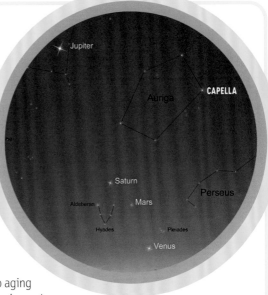

SPOT THIS

LOOK UP INTO THE MILKY WAY TO
SEE BRIGHT STARS OF WINTER,
INCLUDING CAPELLA AT THE TIP
OF THE CONSTELLATION AURIGA.
BELOW AURIGA ARE THE CONSTEL-
LATIONS TAURUS AND ORION.

NAME GAME

Capella plays a key role in the constellation
Auriga the Charioteer. It has its own nickname:
"goat star." Capella represents the goat that is
slung over the chariot driver's shoulder.

Laugh Out Loud!

How do you organize a space
party?

A: You planet!

RIGEL

CLASS B • **MAGNITUDE .12**
• **TEMPERATURE 22,000°F (12,000°C)**
• **DISTANCE FROM EARTH 773**
light-years • **TYPE Multiple**

ORION'S BELT

RIGEL

SPOT THIS RIGEL FORMS THE LEFT FOOT OF THE CON-STELLATION ORION, THE HUNTER. IN WINTER, LOCATE THE THREE STARS OF ORION'S BELT AND FOLLOW THE HIGHEST BELT STAR DOWN ABOUT 45 DEGREES TO THE WEST TO SPOT RIGEL.

Rigel is the brightest star in one of the night sky's most awesome constellations: Orion (see page 72). Rigel also appears in books, movies, and even cartoons. Aliens that abducted members of the Simpson family in one TV episode came from "Rigel IV." (There are actually only three stars in Rigel's multiple-star system.) It also pops up in several *Star Trek* episodes, in Transformers cartoon books, and in video games. Rigel is only ten million years old—that's young for a star—but it's creaking along like a much older star because it's consuming its fuel so fast. Scientists expect Rigel's life to end in a brilliant death called a supernova. The matter in the star will violently collapse inward, releasing an incredible amount of energy. If that happens, Rigel will become the brightest object in the night sky, after the moon.

Did you know?

Rigel's "absolute magnitude"—a measure of how bright the star actually is, not just how bright it appears to us—is about 85,000 times brighter than the sun's. But we see Rigel's "apparent magnitude," which makes it the seventh brightest star in the night sky. That's because star brightness for viewers on Earth depends on their distance from the star. The sun is "only" 93 million miles (150 million km) away from us, whereas Rigel is 773 light-years away. To learn the distance of a light-year, see page 49.

PROCYON

CLASS F · **MAGNITUDE .34**
- **TEMPERATURE 11,300°F (6260°C)**
- **DISTANCE FROM EARTH 11.4 light-years**
- **TYPE Binary**

Procyon and its constellation, Canis Minor (Smaller Dog), is part of a famous winter trio of constellations. Canis Minor and the Larger Dog (Canis Major), trail the hunter Orion through the winter sky. The name Procyon may come from a Greek word that translates as "before the dog," which makes sense because Procyon precedes Sirius the Dog Star each night. Procyon is a binary star, a two-star object. It is among the brightest stars in the northern sky, partly because it is pretty close to Earth, just over 11 light-years away. Compare that to Rigel, which is 773 light-years away and still a very noticeable star in the night sky. Procyon is also a nautical star, one of 57 main sky landmarks that can be used to navigate the oceans.

BETELGEUSE

PROCYON

SIRIUS

SPOT THIS

FIND PROCYON ACROSS FROM BETELGEUSE, THE BRIGHT STAR OF ORION'S RIGHT SHOULDER. THOSE TWO STARS AND SIRIUS FORM THE ASTERISM, OR STAR SHAPE, KNOWN AS THE WINTER TRIANGLE. CHECK OUT THE CHART AT SPACE.COM/22929-PROCYON.HTML.

EXPERT'S CIRCLE

Even though it travels faster than anything else, light still takes time to get from point A to point B. The light we see from Procyon took about 11 years to get here. From Rigel it took 773 years, so we are actually viewing the star the way it looked around A.D. 1300, when there were still knights and castles in some parts of the world.

Laugh Out Loud!

Why didn't the Dog Star laugh at the joke?

A. Because it was too Sirius!

ACHERNAR

CLASS **B** · MAGNITUDE .46 · TEMPERATURE 25,000°F to 34,000°F (14,000° to 19,000°C) · DISTANCE FROM EARTH 114 light-years · TYPE Binary

Achernar is Arabic for "end of the river." This binary star is so far near the bottom of the meandering "river" constellation Eridanus (see page 129) that for a while it was literally off the star map. Some sky charts did not include it because it was not visible north of locations like El Paso in southern Texas. Astronomers know Achernar is there, but it is a mystery. The star spins at a rate of 155 miles (249 km) a second, making it flatten out and bulge at the middle, kind of like a big flying egg. The spin and the shape can't be completely explained by the usual ideas about how stars work, which makes scientists suspect something different may be happening inside Achernar.

Did you know?

Fast-spinning stars like Achernar can get close to what is called "critical rotation." That's the rate at which they spin so fast that their internal gravity can't hold them together and they break apart.

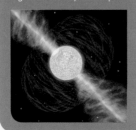

CHANCES OF SEEING EGG-SHAPED ACHERNAR (TOP) FROM THE UNITED STATES ARE PRETTY SMALL, UNLESS YOU'RE SOUTH OF MIAMI, FLORIDA. FOLLOW THE RIVER CONSTELLATION ERIDANUS. AT ITS END IS ACHERNAR (ABOVE). FIND OUT MORE AT EARTHSKY.ORG/BRIGHTEST-STARS/BRIGHT-ACHERNAR-ENDS-THE-SOUTHERN-RIVER.

NAME GAME

We often think of astronomy as the "invention" of the ancient Greeks because of their discoveries. Also, the planets are named after the gods of ancient Greece and Rome. But many of the stars were named by early Arab astronomers, who also made numerous discoveries.

NOVAE

Most binary stars are in balance with each other. They are often the same type of star and are just close enough or far enough apart to unite around a common point of gravity. If they didn't, they would either crash into each other or drift apart. But sometimes the two stars age at different rates. If one has already collapsed to form a white dwarf and the other is in red giant stage, the scene is set for a nova (plural: novae)—a nuclear explosion on a cosmic scale. As the red giant expands, the other star will start drawing away hydrogen gas from the red giant. (The "pull," above, looks like a string of taffy.) When that cloud of gas becomes large and dense enough, it can explode, becoming a nova. Sometimes it happens with such force that a star we don't usually see on Earth becomes visible to the naked eye. Some binary pairs go through this cycle several times.

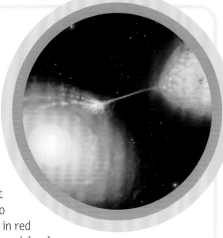

NOVAE ARE RARE, BUT THEY MAY BE SEEN IN OR NEAR THE MILKY WAY IN HUBBLE SPACE TELESCOPE PHOTOS (ABOVE) AT HUBBLESITE.ORG/NEWSCENTER/ARCHIVE/RELEASES/STAR/NOVA/2004/10/.

TRY THIS!

Heat and pressure make things expand, and stars are no different. With a parent's permission and help, put a marshmallow in your microwave. Cook for about 30 seconds and keep an eye on it. (Press "Stop" immediately if you think the marshmallow is going to explode!) What do you think is happening?

A variable star is any star that changes in brightness as seen from Earth. The brightness change may be caused by processes within the star as it grows older. Or two stars may be in orbit around each other so that one star eclipses the other periodically.

EXPERT'S CIRCLE

SUPERNOVAE

Supernovae occur in a way similar to novae. The core of a white dwarf star can take in so much extra hydrogen that it implodes, or collapses inward, starting a violent explosion. The same thing can also happen to a red supergiant star. A difference between a nova and supernova is the power of the explosion. For a short time, a supernova can release as much energy as all the stars in the Milky Way! The explosion also creates raw materials for the formation of future stars. Another difference is that a supernova can happen only once in the life of a star. The transformation of a founding star's material is permanent. But a star can experience a nova event more than once in its lifetime.

Did you know?

The bright flash of a supernova can often be seen with the naked eye. The Chinese were the first to record the spotting of a supernova in A.D. 185. The brightest supernova in recent years occurred in 1987.

SPOT THIS

A NASA IMAGE (TOP) SHOWS THE REMAINS OF A SUPERNOVA THAT EXPLODED IN A GALAXY NEXT TO THE MILKY WAY. THE BLUE GAS HERE AND IN THE CRAB NEBULA (ABOVE) IS MANY MILLIONS OF DEGREES HOT.

be a SKYWATCHER!

LOOK FOR THIS! The Crab Nebula, located in the constellation Taurus (see page 91), is the leftover remains of a supernova that exploded almost a thousand years ago. Back then, the star that produced this cloud of expanding gases was visible to the eye for almost two years.

BLACK HOLES

Some supernovae become star nurseries, full of the raw materials for star formation. Other supernovae seem to disappear. The last explosive moments of a supernova can create such strong gravity that all the matter from the explosion collapses inward, creating a black hole. It's called that because gravity squeezes the particles of matter so tightly that there is no space

between them. Not even a tiny glimmer of light can escape a black hole's gravity! But if there's nothing to see, how do scientists know black holes are there? They know because black holes gobble up the stars around them, causing stellar gases to swirl like a whirlpool into the black hole. Then they're gone. Stars can't just vanish, though. They have to be somewhere—and that somewhere is tightly squeezed into a black hole. Black holes often exist in the center of galaxies.

A BLACK HOLE CAN'T BE SEEN BECAUSE ITS INTENSE GRAVITY DOES NOT LET LIGHT ESCAPE. IF IT WERE VISIBLE, YOU MIGHT SEE A BIG SWIRL OF GASES, AS IN THIS ART (RIGHT AND TOP).

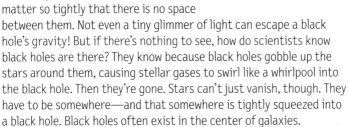

SPOT THIS

EXPERT'S CIRCLE

Black holes formed by single stars are the most common type. There may be a few billion of them in the Milky Way galaxy alone. Some galaxies, like the Milky Way, seem to be centered around supermassive black holes. These are thought to be formed by clusters of stars that die and compact together. Then they sink to the center of a galaxy and collect with other dead clusters in a giant black hole.

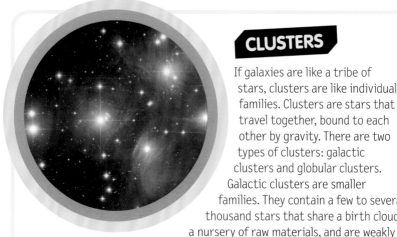

CLUSTERS

If galaxies are like a tribe of stars, clusters are like individual families. Clusters are stars that travel together, bound to each other by gravity. There are two types of clusters: galactic clusters and globular clusters. Galactic clusters are smaller families. They contain a few to several thousand stars that share a birth cloud, a nursery of raw materials, and are weakly bound together by gravity. A good example of a galactic cluster is the Pleiades in the constellation Taurus (above and on pages 102–103). Globular clusters are generally round and supersize. They can contain a million or more stars that also share a birth cloud. Some clusters can be seen with the naked eye. One is the Hyades, also in Taurus (see page 91). The Beehive cluster is located in the constellation Cancer (see page 93), and Coma Berenices is in the constellation with the same name (see page 118).

Did you know?

Star clusters show how galaxies can collide and rob each other of stars. A globular cluster in the Milky Way known as M79 occurs away from our galaxy's center, where other globular clusters usually are found. It was likely stolen from a nearby dwarf galaxy that is slowly being absorbed by the Milky Way.

SPOT THIS

GLOBULAR CLUSTER OMEGA CENTAURI (ABOVE), WITH SOME TEN MILLION STARS, IS FOUND IN THE SOUTHERN-SKY CONSTELLATION CENTAURUS.

be a SKYWATCHER!

LOOK FOR THIS! In summer, search around the constellation Sagittarius for globular clusters that occur within the galactic core of our Milky Way galaxy. Some of these clusters, such as M22 or M28, can be seen with the naked eye or binoculars.

NEBULAE

A nebula is a cloud nursery where new stars are formed. Most nebulae (pronounced NEB-you-lee) are the remains of a super-nova rich in hydrogen, helium, and other elements. Scientists think that the first nebulae were created at the big bang, the cosmic event that started the formation of our universe. It also began the star- and planet-forming processes that continue today. You can see nebulae with a four-inch

(10-cm) or six-inch (15-cm) telescope, but you will get a better look by using a larger telescope with light filters that make the details stand out more clearly. The Orion Nebula is a good place to start your nebula watch. Located 1,500 light-years from Earth, it can be seen with the naked eye (or binoculars) on a clear, dark winter night below Orion's belt.

SPOT THIS

A NEBULA CAN APPEAR AS A FUZZY STAR TO THE NAKED EYE. THE HELIX NEBULA (ABOVE) CAN BE SPOTTED WITH BINOCULARS IN THE CONSTELLATION AQUARIUS (SEE PAGE 100). THE HUBBLE SPACE TELESCOPE CAPTURED THE AWESOME SHAPE OF THE HORSEHEAD NEBULA IN ORION (TOP), WHICH GIVES OFF NO LIGHT OF ITS OWN BUT IS SILHOUETTED AGAINST A BRIGHTER NEBULA.

Did you know?

Scientists have used the Hubble Space Telescope to get a close-up view of the Orion Nebula. It has given us amazing views of all the stages of star formation— and a look at the beginnings of new solar systems!

be a SKYWATCHER!

LOOK FOR THIS! Below the middle of Orion's belt (see page 72) lies the Orion Nebula. Under the right conditions and with sharp eyes, you can detect its fuzziness. A telescope will show its four brightest stars, known as the Trapezium for the shape they make.

Spectacular Sky:
Eagle Nebula

About 7,000 light-years from Earth, the Eagle Nebula has a lot going on. It is both a nebula and a star cluster—and the site of a lot of star-forming activity. You can find the Eagle Nebula in the tail portion of the constellation Serpens. Binoculars and low-powered telescopes will give you a look at some stars and haze. An eight-inch (20-cm) or larger telescope will reveal the shape of an eagle with its wings spread that gives the nebula its name. But if you want to see the Eagle Nebula at its best, check out the images captured by the Hubble Space Telescope (hubblesite.org)!

Serpens

Serpens the Serpent is
the only constellation in
the sky that is split in two.
Its head appears in one place
and its tail in another. Look for
Serpens in June and July by facing
south and locating the constellation Ophiuchus
the Serpent Bearer (see page 138). The snake's
triangular head lies to the west and points up
with a pair of stars forming a forked "tongue."
Its tail appears to the east of Ophiuchus as a
long L-shape of stars.

Pillars of Creation

At the center of the Eagle Nebula rise three
dark pillars of dense material that can be seen
with a 12-inch (30-cm) telescope. But this view
will be nothing compared to the famous images
of the Pillars of Creation on the Hubble website.
Newborn stars sculpted the pillars by burning
away some of their gases. Here's a mind-boggling
thought: Scientists think a supernova destroyed the pillars
6,000 years ago, but we haven't received the evidence yet. The light
from the supernova won't arrive in our sky for hundreds of years!

Seasons of the Sky

The constellation Orion sparkling in the winter sky

In this section you'll look at the sky during different seasons of the year—winter, spring, summer, and autumn—and discover stars and star shapes especially visible in each season.

From the beginning of skywatching, humans have recognized star patterns and made up stories to explain them. We call major recognized star patterns constellations. Smaller recognized patterns are known as asterisms. Asterisms occur within constellations or connect stars in different constellations. Both constellations and asterisms help skywatchers locate stars and other objects near them.

On pages 68 through 85, you'll find sky charts for each season. First choose the appropriate chart for your current season. Try to use it at the time indicated in the table at the top right of the chart. Turn the map so the direction you are facing appears right side up, then use it to help locate constellations and other objects.

In the spreads following each seasonal sky chart are entries for constellations or asterisms that are easy to see in that season. Vital information gives the number of main stars in the star pattern, how wide it stretches across the sky (using your hands and fists to measure), and what months of the year it is easiest to see.

The word "constellation" doesn't refer only to the star shapes themselves, but also to a recognized area of the sky around them. These sky neighborhoods include star clusters, nebulae, and galaxies. Using neighborhoods helps astronomers describe where other sky objects are located, such as the Andromeda galaxy (see pages 120–121)—which is seen in the same part of the sky as the constellation Andromeda (see page 106). This galaxy, however, is not close by in distance. Instead, it is a deep-sky object.

On all the star charts, deep-sky objects have numbers that begin with M or NGC. M stands for the name of Charles Messier, the French astronomer who created a catalog of deep-sky objects in the 1700s. The objects' names range from M1 to M110. For instance, M1 is the Crab Nebula (see page 91). A larger catalog, which has some of the same objects in Messier's catalog, is the New General Catalogue, started by astronomer John Herschel in the 1800s. It is still being updated. Its objects carry the letters NGC, such as the Intergalactic Wanderer, NGC 2419 (see page 135). Finally, you'll see Greek letters next to stars on many constellations. Astronomers use these to rank the stars in that constellation from brightest, alpha (∂), to the least bright, omega (Ω).

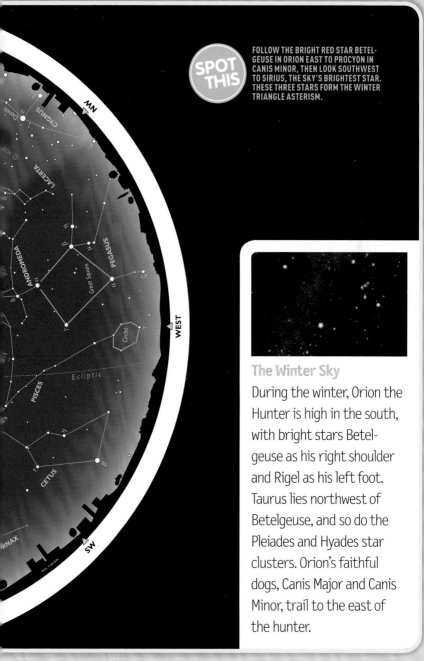

SPOT THIS

FOLLOW THE BRIGHT RED STAR BETELGEUSE IN ORION EAST TO PROCYON IN CANIS MINOR, THEN LOOK SOUTHWEST TO SIRIUS, THE SKY'S BRIGHTEST STAR. THESE THREE STARS FORM THE WINTER TRIANGLE ASTERISM.

The Winter Sky

During the winter, Orion the Hunter is high in the south, with bright stars Betelgeuse as his right shoulder and Rigel as his left foot. Taurus lies northwest of Betelgeuse, and so do the Pleiades and Hyades star clusters. Orion's faithful dogs, Canis Major and Canis Minor, trail to the east of the hunter.

THE BIG DIPPER

MAKEUP 7 stars · BEST VIEWED Year-round · LOCATION Rotates overhead throughout the year · ALPHA STAR Alioth · SIZE

The Big Dipper may be the most famous shape in the northern sky. The seven stars of this asterism form an unmistakable ladle—or dipper—with the two stars on the outside of the ladle's bowl pointing directly to Polaris, the North Star. The Big Dipper is part of the constellation Ursa Major (Great Bear). But other cultures see different shapes in the Big Dipper. To some, it is a giant farm plow or a cart, to others a meat cleaver or even a group of heavenly wise men. Across the northern part of the world, the Big Dipper is a constant companion. It is located so close to the celestial north pole that it is visible year-round. Because it never dips below the horizon, it is always visible in the northern sky, where skywatchers in North America will see it. It simply rotates overhead through the seasons. In spring, it is high in the sky and upside down, as if it were dumping its water out. In the fall, it is closer to the horizon and right-side up. In summer and winter, it faces to the side. The Big Dipper is such a constant in the sky that escaped slaves who traveled along the Under-

EXPERT'S CIRCLE

The Big Dipper is the first star shape that many kids learn, but it is not a constellation. Instead, the Big Dipper is an asterism, a small collection of stars that form a distinctive shape. It happens to be located within and is part of the constellation Ursa Major (left). Many asterism shapes are geometric, like triangles or squares. Asterisms may include stars from more than one constellation. Their shapes help people find their way around the sky.

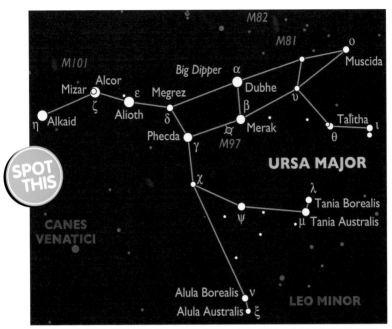

THE BIG DIPPER, AN ASTERISM IN THE URSA MAJOR CONSTELLATION, IS VISIBLE YEAR-ROUND IF YOU FACE THE NORTH HORIZON. BUT IT IS BEST VIEWED IN THE SPRING, WHEN IT IS ALMOST DIRECTLY OVERHEAD.

ground Railroad used it to reach northern states and freedom. They mentioned the Big Dipper in their stories and songs, including "Follow the Drinking Gourd."

be a SKYWATCHER!

LOOK FOR THIS! Polaris, in the handle of the Little Dipper, is not the brightest star in the sky. But it is still one of the most important stars because it lets people figure out where they are going by showing them the direction north. For thousands of years, travelers, navigators, and explorers have counted on Polaris to show them the way.

Did you know?

Most of the stars of the Big Dipper form a small cluster that is stuck together by gravity, so the stars are moving together in the same direction. That means the pattern they form today will be almost the same 100,000 years from now.

ORION THE HUNTER

MAKEUP 20 stars · **BEST VIEWED** January and February · **LOCATION** Winter, southeast · **ALPHA STAR** Betelgeuse · **SIZE**

Winter brings the constellation Orion into the spotlight, so it's easy to locate from the three close diagonal stars of its belt. Checking out Orion's other stars, you can use your imagination to see the rest of the hunter. The towering giant holds a club in one hand and a lion's pelt in the other (see page 66). Ancient Syrians called the constellation Al Jabar, the Giant. Two of the brightest stars in the sky, Rigel and Betelgeuse, shine from Orion's left foot and right shoulder like giant jewels (see top, opposite).

It's no wonder that peoples all over the world have pondered Orion for millennia, creating myths about the constellation and making it part of human history. Orion is mentioned in the Bible and in the famous Greek poems *The Iliad* and *The Odyssey*. In one Greek myth, Orion is stung by the scorpion of the nearby constellation Scorpius (see page 97). In another, he is killed by the goddess Artemis, who was tricked into shooting him with a poisoned arrow. Now he lights up the night sky and helps skywatchers find their way in the company of his nearby dogs, Canis Major and Canis Minor (see pages 113, 114).

To enjoy the sky around Orion, focus on Rigel on Orion's left foot. It sits at the top of Eridanus, the River, a long constellation whose end may dip

EXPERT'S CIRCLE

In the early 17th century, German astronomer Johann Bayer came up with a way to clearly describe the brightness of the stars in constellations by using Greek letters. He used the alpha symbol for the brightest star, the beta symbol for the second brightest, and so on. But here's a puzzle: If Rigel is Orion's brightest star, why is it named Beta Orionis, instead of Alpha Orionis? It may be because Bayer was working at a time when Betelgeuse happened to shine brighter than Rigel. As a variable star, Betelgeuse sometimes shines more brightly than at other times.

below the horizon and not be visible. North of Betelgeuse, find the rectangle of Gemini the Twins (see page 92), marked by the stars Castor and Pollux. Now move west and pick out the bright star Capella. It's the marker for the constellation Auriga (see page 109). Farther west—and north—look for six stars that form a crooked W or M, depending on your location (find all these on pages 68–69). That's Cassiopeia, a queen from Greek mythology (see page 84). Looking even farther west, you'll find the famous winged horse Pegasus (see page 83), whose body is formed by a bright, four-star asterism known as the Great Square.

NAME GAME

One of Orion's stars, Bellatrix, lent its name to the wild character Bellatrix Lestrange in the Harry Potter books.

be a SKYWATCHER!

LOOK FOR THIS! The part of the Milky Way where Orion is located is a ginormous star nursery. To find it, look for three stars hanging from Orion's belt that form his sword. Here you'll find the Orion Nebula (M42), which is visible with the naked eye or binoculars. At its center is the Trapezium asterism. Inside the nebula, stars are beginning to form.

Did you know?

Betelgeuse may have only a million years left before it explodes in a supernova. In the meantime, it is swelling and shrinking like a balloon, with a diameter that changes from 550 to 920 times as large as the sun's.

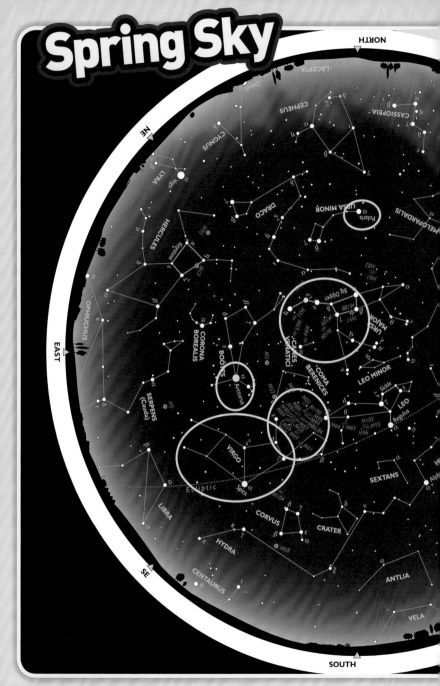

Spring Sky

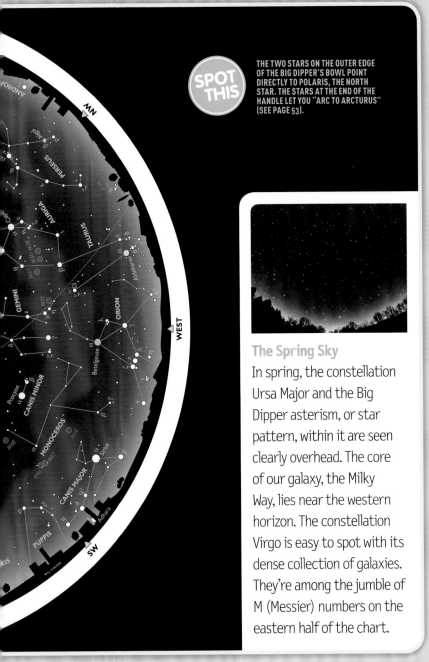

SPOT THIS

THE TWO STARS ON THE OUTER EDGE OF THE BIG DIPPER'S BOWL POINT DIRECTLY TO POLARIS, THE NORTH STAR. THE STARS AT THE END OF THE HANDLE LET YOU "ARC TO ARCTURUS" (SEE PAGE 53).

The Spring Sky

In spring, the constellation Ursa Major and the Big Dipper asterism, or star pattern, within it are seen clearly overhead. The core of our galaxy, the Milky Way, lies near the western horizon. The constellation Virgo is easy to spot with its dense collection of galaxies. They're among the jumble of M (Messier) numbers on the eastern half of the chart.

VITALS Leo the Lion
MAKEUP **12 stars** · BEST VIEWED **March and April**
· LOCATION **Spring, center of chart**
· ALPHA STAR **Regulus** · SIZE ✋
VITALS Leo Minor
MAKEUP **3 stars** · BEST VIEWED **March and April**
· LOCATION **Spring, center of chart** · ALPHA STAR
None (beta star: Beta Leonis Minoris) · SIZE ✋

Leo the Lion is most visible in the spring, just as the bright stars of winter begin to fade and before the summer view of the Milky Way becomes brightest. In March and April, you'll find Leo directly below the Big Dipper. You can imagine the dipper pouring water on the lion's head!

Leo is one of the oldest and most recognizable constellations. In mythology it represents the Nemean lion, one of the animals that Hercules was tasked to kill as part of his 12 labors. Leo may even have been a high-in-the-sky model for the ancient Egyptians when they designed their famous Sphinx, the massive stone lion with a human head built near the Great Pyramids of Giza. Leo Minor (Small Lion) is less noticeable. Its stars are so faint that the pattern is hard to see from many locations. It was added to sky charts as a constellation in the 17th century.

Leo itself stands in a fairly empty patch of the spring sky. Its head is known as the Sickle, an asterism like the Big Dipper that ends with the bright star Regulus.

Did you know?

Leo Minor may be seen as a little lion today, but to the ancient Egyptians this group of stars near Leo represented a herd of gazelles that were trying to run away from a hungry lion.

R LEONIS
REGULUS

EXPERT'S CIRCLE

Near the bright blue star Regulus near Leo's head, look for the variable star R Leonis, which is deep orange-red in color. Use it to practice watching how variable stars change over time. You'll need binoculars to check on this star every two weeks. Try to notice its changes in brightness for about ten months, if you can.

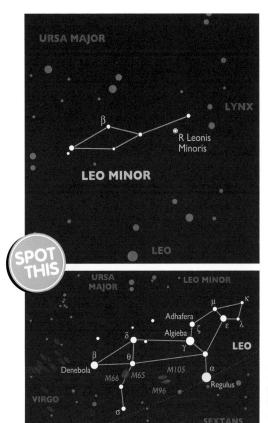

LEO MINOR

URSA MAJOR

LYNX

β

R Leonis Minoris

LEO

URSA MAJOR — LEO MINOR

μ κ
Adhafera
ζ ε λ
δ Algieba
γ **LEO**
β θ
Denebola
M66 M65 M105 α
M96 Regulus

VIRGO

σ

SEXTANS

See the rest of the spring sky by looking below Regulus. You'll find the triangular head of Hydra, the serpent whose snaky body straddles the spring night. Virgo, a place to spot distant galaxies, comes into view in the east. To the west you can find Orion, which gradually grows dimmer and will move out of sight with the coming of summer.

TO FIND LEO AND LEO MINOR, USE THE CHART ON PAGES 74–75 TO LOOK DOWN FROM THE BIG DIPPER'S HANDLE, MOVE EAST TO ARCTURUS, "SPEED TO SPICA," AND THEN TURN WEST TO FIND REGULUS AND ITS CONSTELLATION LEO.

SPOT THIS

be a SKYWATCHER!

LOOK FOR THIS! November brings the Leonid meteor showers that seem to streak from the area of the constellation Leo. The best way to view the showers is far from city lights, between midnight and dawn. Be sure to stay warm, and view the showers with a parent or other trusted adult.

Summer Sky

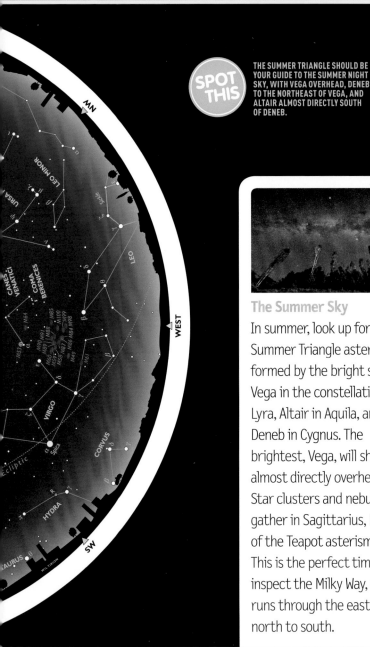

SPOT THIS

THE SUMMER TRIANGLE SHOULD BE YOUR GUIDE TO THE SUMMER NIGHT SKY, WITH VEGA OVERHEAD, DENEB TO THE NORTHEAST OF VEGA, AND ALTAIR ALMOST DIRECTLY SOUTH OF DENEB.

The Summer Sky

In summer, look up for the Summer Triangle asterism, formed by the bright stars Vega in the constellation Lyra, Altair in Aquila, and Deneb in Cygnus. The brightest, Vega, will shine almost directly overhead. Star clusters and nebulae gather in Sagittarius, home of the Teapot asterism. This is the perfect time to inspect the Milky Way, which runs through the east from north to south.

SUMMER TRIANGLE

MAKEUP 3 stars · **BEST VIEWED** Summer · **LOCATION**
Summer, east · **SIZE**

Summer may be the best season to learn to navigate the sky. The nights are warm and the Earth looks out to the thick center of the Milky Way (left), bringing a crowded group of constellations and other objects into view. The tour starts with the Summer Triangle. This is an easy shape to find. It's not a constellation, but an asterism, a recognizable star shape. Its three stars are Deneb in the constellation Cygnus the Swan (see page 125), Vega in Lyra the Lyre (see page 136), and Altair in the constellation Aquila the Eagle (see page 108). From a dark location in good conditions, the triangle is also your window on a part of the Milky Way that is dense with stars and other sky objects. Think of the galaxy as a river of stars. Deneb sits in the middle and the river flows between Vega and Altair, now directly overhead. The nearby stars form Lyra, one of the few northern constellations named for an object instead of an animal or mythical figure. Just to the north, Draco the Dragon (see page 127), rears its

NAME GAME

The Summer Triangle hasn't been a big part of the history of astronomy. In fact, the name was made up in the 1950s by a radio broadcaster. He used the term to help people find their way around the sky—and it stuck!

TRY THIS!

Because it is so bright and easy to find, the Summer Triangle is a good way to see how the sky changes over the year. Watch for the triangle in the east during the spring and mark its travels west through the summer and into fall. Notice the constellations that travel with it and how they change position too.

IN THE SUMMER TRIANGLE, VEGA IS BLAZING RIGHT OVERHEAD AND DENEB IS JUST A BIT TO THE EAST. FROM THERE DRAW A LINE TO ALTAIR. LOOK AROUND THE STARS OF THE SUMMER TRIANGLE TO SEE THEIR FULL CONSTELLATIONS: CYGNUS THE SWAN, LYRA THE LYRE, AND AQUILA THE EAGLE.

head. Hercules (see page 131) is directly to the south. West of Hercules, the bright star Arcturus leads you to the kite-shaped Boötes the Herdsman (see page 110).

Meanwhile, Pegasus has risen in the east. But don't forget to look south, where Sagittarius the Archer will point the way to thick clusters of stars and nebulae in the heart of the Milky Way. Near Sagittarius, the serpent bearer Ophiuchus (see page 138) and the two-part snake constellation Serpens wind across the sky.

be a SKYWATCHER!

LOOK FOR THIS! Giant Deneb is among the most distant stars you can see with the naked eye. It is more than 1,500 light-years away, so you are seeing it as it was during the Dark Ages, about 500 B.C. We see it only because it's so bright, about 60,000 times as bright as the sun.

Did you know?

Vega is among the closest of the bright stars, only 25.3 light-years away. In 1850, Vega was the first star to be photographed after the sun.

Autumn Sky

NORTH

URSA MAJOR
Big Dipper

DRACO

NE

LYNX

GEMINI

M81
M82

CAMELOPARDALIS

AURIGA

Capella

URSA MINOR

Polaris α

DRACO

CEPHEUS

CASSIOPEIA

Double Cluster

PERSEUS

Algol

LACERTA

M34

M52

Andromeda

TRIANGULUM

M31 M110 M32

ANDROMEDA

Aldebaran

ORION

δ ε Hyades

Pleiades

M33

α

EAST

TAURUS

η

ARIES

γ

β

M74

α

PEGASUS

α

Great Square

M15

EQUULEUS

M2

β

PISCES

Ecliptic

Water Jug

ERIDANUS

Mira

Circlet

AQUARIUS

δ

CETUS

τ

β

M30

CAPRICORNUS

SE

FORNAX

Fomalhaut

α

SCULPTOR

PISCIS
AUSTRINUS

γ

PHOENIX

α

GRUS

β

α

SOUTH

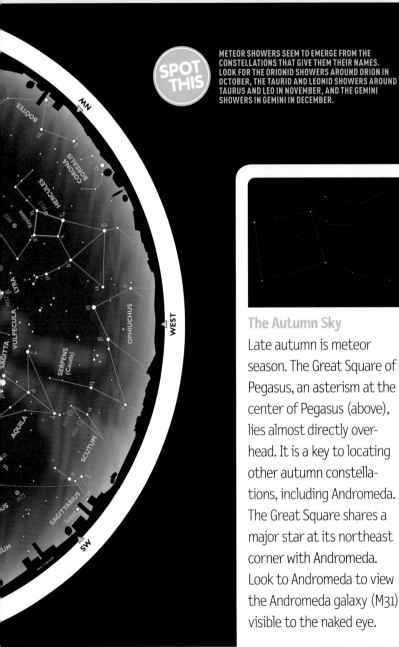

METEOR SHOWERS SEEM TO EMERGE FROM THE CONSTELLATIONS THAT GIVE THEM THEIR NAMES. LOOK FOR THE ORIONID SHOWERS AROUND ORION IN OCTOBER, THE TAURID AND LEONID SHOWERS AROUND TAURUS AND LEO IN NOVEMBER, AND THE GEMINI SHOWERS IN GEMINI IN DECEMBER.

The Autumn Sky

Late autumn is meteor season. The Great Square of Pegasus, an asterism at the center of Pegasus (above), lies almost directly overhead. It is a key to locating other autumn constellations, including Andromeda. The Great Square shares a major star at its northeast corner with Andromeda. Look to Andromeda to view the Andromeda galaxy (M31), visible to the naked eye.

CASSIOPEIA

MAKEUP 5 stars · **BEST VIEWED** October and November · **LOCATION** Autumn, northeast quadrant · **ALPHA STAR** Shedar · **SIZE**

In Greek mythology, a proud queen of Ethiopia, Cassiopeia, bragged that her daughter Andromeda was more beautiful than the daughters of the sea god Nereus. For that, the chief sea god, Poseidon, chained her to a throne and placed her in the sky, where she is sometimes forced to hang upside down. The five-star constellation is one of the highlights of the autumn sky. There is a whole cast of characters in Cassiopeia's family story, which involves a set of five constellations. Learning the tale is a good way to understand the sky as the leaves begin to turn.

In the fall, you'll find Cassiopeia in the northeast, swimming in the Milky Way with her W shape pointing toward Polaris. Her husband Cepheus is just to the west, her daughter Andromeda is to the east, and the hero Perseus is to the north. He rode the winged Pegasus to save Andromeda from death.

Plan ahead to November and December for good locations to watch yearly meteor shows. Surrounding Cassiopeia at this time, you'll find Perseus to the east. Andromeda and giant Pegasus are to the south. Cepheus is still to the west.

The Summer Triangle has now moved west but remains visible for part of the night, and you may still need its bright stars for reference points. Unlike in the summer, when many of the brightest stars

GAMMA CASSIOPEIA

EXPERT'S CIRCLE

The star in the middle of Cassiopeia is an irregular variable star called Gamma (γ) Cassiopeia. It follows no particular cycle as it shines brightly and then grows dim. Unpredictably, it became so bright for a while that it was the brightest star in the constellation. It even outshone brighter stars like Deneb.

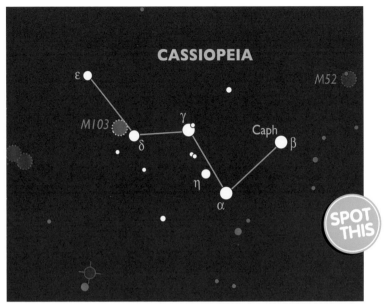

CASSIOPEIA

ε
M52
M103
γ
Caph
δ
β
η
α

SPOT THIS

IF CASSIOPEIA'S GIANT W DOESN'T STAND OUT WHERE YOU ARE, FIND VEGA, WHICH HAS NOW MOVED TO THE WEST, AND START LOOKING EAST FROM THERE. CASSIOPEIA APPEARS IN THE NORTHEASTERN SKY IN THE MIDDLE OF THE MILKY WAY, WHICH FLOWS DOWN TO THE SOUTHWEST.

are visible together, the fall constellations are made up of dimmer stars. But there are still some great sights. To the south, the "water" constellations are coming into view: Pisces the Fish (see page 101), the water bearer Aquarius (see page 100), and the sea monster Cetus (see page 116). And the river Eridanus (see page 129) is just flowing into sight.

Did you know?

If you found yourself on Alpha Centauri, the closest star to the sun, and wanted to find Earth, you'd simply look toward Cassiopeia.

NAME GAME

Cassiopeia is a good example of how Arab, Chinese, Greek, and other astronomers developed their own descriptions of the sky. Arab astronomers saw a camel in Cassiopeia. One of its stars was called Al Sanam al Nakah, the Camel's Hump. Chinese astronomers named it the Bridge of Kings.

Spectacular Sky: Southern Sky Stars

It's fun to think that everyone on Earth shares a view of the moon and that kids in China or Nigeria see the same sky object as kids in the United States or Canada. Many constellations can be seen at least part of the year no matter where you live on the planet. But there are a bunch of stars, constellations, and other sky objects that you can see only if you travel far enough south—to Mexico or Argentina or across the Southern Pacific Ocean. The night sky of the Southern Hemisphere contains an array of stars, clusters, nebulae, and galaxies that mostly are seen only there. Many were given names in more modern times than objects in northern skies, and the names often honor the tools of science and art.

Magellanic Clouds

The Large and Small Magellanic Clouds are small galaxies known as irregular dwarf galaxies that orbit the Milky Way. Astronomers once thought that these galaxies were native to the Milky Way, but they recently discovered that they began in deep space and journeyed to their present orbits.

Crux the Southern Cross

The most famous constellation in the southern sky is Crux, the Southern Cross. It's the smallest constellation—composed of four stars—but it's bright and has guided sailors in southern seas for thousands of years. Crux contains the Jewel Box galactic cluster as well as the Coalsack Nebula, a dense cloud of gas and dust.

Centaurus

Centaurus is a huge constellation that includes the bright star Alpha Centauri, the sun's close neighbor at only 4.4 light-years away. Centaurus is probably named for Chiron, the half man, half horse who tutored many figures in Greek mythology, including Hercules. Centaurus is located in the southern sky just above Crux.

The Zodiac

ARIES

PISCES

AQUARIUS

CAPRICORN

SAGITTARIUS

SCORPIO

LIBRA

This zodiac circle shows the zodiac constellations and their symbols.

GEMINI

CANCER

LEO

EXPERT'S CIRCLE

Imagine a carousel of beautiful animals and figures traveling across the night sky in a procession that takes a year to complete. That's the zodiac, a word of Greek origin for "circle of animals." In the pages to follow you will discover the 12 constellations of the zodiac. They move along an imaginary line called the ecliptic. The line traces the apparent path taken by the sun across the sky. The constellations of the zodiac are a special group of star shapes that have been watched and described for thousands of years. They form the basis of the astrological "signs" that some cultures have used to explain or predict events.

You've probably heard of astronomy and astrology, but what's the difference? Astronomy is a science based on facts or ideas that can be tested by experiments and then accepted or rejected based on the results. Astronomy has been studied since ancient times. In the history of astronomy, ideas once thought to be true—like the idea that the sun revolved around the Earth—were proven false and rejected. Astrology is a pseudoscience, or "fake" science. It may seem organized and factual, but it does not rely on experiments to prove or disprove things. The predictions astrologers make about what will happen to a person based on the "sign" or constellation for his or her month of birth are not science, but they are often entertaining!

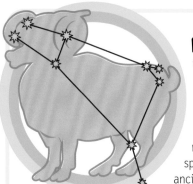

ARIES THE RAM

VITALS Aries the Ram ▪ **MAKEUP** 4 stars ▪ **BEST VIEWED** November and December ▪ **LOCATION** Winter, southwest quadrant ▪ **ALPHA STAR** Hamal ▪ **SIZE** 🖐

By tradition, the zodiac starts with Aries, the constellation that inaugurated spring in the Northern Hemisphere thousands of years ago. The ancient astronomers who came up with the circle of animals noticed that the sun set near Aries on the day of the vernal equinox, spring's official beginning. That's the day when the sun crosses the celestial equator. Equinox means "equal night," or that the day is almost equally divided between sunlight and darkness. The wobble of the Earth as it spins on its axis changes Aries to a different position on the first day of spring. But Aries is still used as the starting point for the zodiac's annual cycle. Four main stars stand out in the brightest part of this constellation, which represents the source of the Golden Fleece stolen by Jason and the Argonauts in Greek mythology. In the myth, Aries was sent to rescue two children from their dangerous stepmother. When the ram returned, it was sacrificed in honor of Zeus. The animal's furry skin, the Golden Fleece, was placed in a sacred tomb. Jason later stole it on his epic journey with the Argonauts.

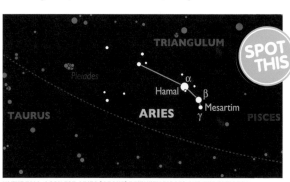

IN THE FALL, LOOK FOR ARIES (ABOVE) BETWEEN PISCES AND THE PLEIADES.

Did you know?

In 1664, astronomer Robert Hooke was the first to view through a telescope the double star Mesartim, one of the main stars in the constellation Aries.

TAURUS THE BULL

VITALS Taurus the Bull • MAKEUP 13 stars • BEST VIEWED January
and February • LOCATION Winter, southwest quadrant
• ALPHA STAR Aldebaran • SIZE 🖐

Taurus is a mega constellation with a
shape that really does look like a bull.
Starting with the alpha star Aldebaran,
its horns jut out into space to the east,
while its body trails behind. Ancient peoples
saw these stars as a bull for as long as 5,000
years, making Taurus one of the oldest identified
shapes in the sky. Back then, bulls often were given godlike status. For
the Greeks, the Taurus bull represented their great god Zeus. According
to myth, Zeus turned himself into a white bull to attract the beautiful
Europa, who lived near the Mediterranean Sea. Kneeling before her, he
got Europa to climb onto his back. As soon as she did, he sped to Crete,
part of Europe. Zeus transformed back into himself and kept Europa with
him on the continent
that would bear her
name—Europe.

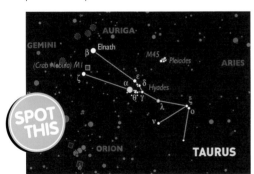

SPOT THIS

THE STARS OF ORION'S BELT POINT NORTHWEST TO ALDEBARAN,
THE BULL'S ALPHA STAR.

be a SKYWATCHER!

LOOK FOR THIS! Taurus contains two major star
clusters—the Pleiades and the Hyades—that really
stand out in the winter night sky. A telescope will show
the Crab Nebula, the bright remains of a supernova that
exploded in 1054. It was the first object that astronomer
Charles Messier put in his catalog of deep-sky objects.
That's why its Messier number is M1.

Did you know?

The supernova that caused
the Crab Nebula (M1) was at
first so bright that it was visible
to the naked eye. Historical
records suggest it may have
been visible during the day for
about a month.

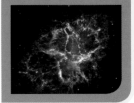

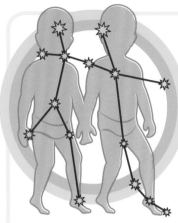

GEMINI THE TWINS

VITALS **Gemini the Twins** · MAKEUP **13 stars** · BEST VIEWED **February and March** · LOCATION **Winter, southeast quadrant** · ALPHA STAR **Castor** · SIZE 🖐

The name Gemini is Latin for "twins." At the top of the Gemini constellation, the two bright stars Castor and Pollux mark the heads of a famous set of twins from Greek mythology. They are the sons of Leda and the god Zeus, as well as of Leda's human husband. Castor was considered the mortal twin and Pollux the immortal one, with Zeus as his father. When Castor was killed in battle, Pollux asked to give up his immortality to join him in death, and the pair were set in the sky as a memorial so that they could always be together. The brothers remain close, shining brightly and hanging near the dome of the sky. Gemini is visible to skywatchers for about half of the year.

SPOT THIS

TO LOCATE GEMINI (ABOVE), LOOK JUST NORTHEAST OF BETELGEUSE, THE BRIGHT STAR AT THE SHOULDER OF ORION.

be a SKYWATCHER!

LOOK FOR THIS! Looking through a telescope, you'll see Castor as a double star. But it actually has several partner stars. These include Castor B, Castor C, and a few red dwarf stars.

CANCER THE CRAB

VITALS Cancer the Crab · **MAKEUP** 5 stars · **BEST VIEWED** March and April · **LOCATION** Spring, southwest quadrant · **ALPHA STAR** Acubens · **SIZE**

The five stars of Cancer don't shine as brightly as those of other zodiac constellations. But what it lacks in bright stars, Cancer makes up for with several star clusters. The dense Beehive cluster (M44) can be seen with the naked eye on a dark night. The galactic cluster M67 contains about 500 stars and can be spotted with a small telescope. Cancer's mythological story involves Hercules, the superhero who was the son of Zeus and a mortal woman. Zeus's wife, the goddess Hera, was always annoyed by Hercules and made life hard for him. When Hercules battled the multiheaded monster Hydra as one of his 12 labors, Hera sent a crab to pinch him on the foot and distract him. But the crab was no match for Hercules. It died under Hercules' heel, earning a place in the stars.

CANCER (ABOVE) CRAWLS BETWEEN CONSTELLATIONS GEMINI AND LEO AND LIES JUST ABOVE THE HEAD OF HYDRA.

be a SKYWATCHER!

LOOK FOR THIS! The Beehive cluster lies right in the middle of Cancer. While visible to the naked eye under the right conditions, binoculars will bring it easily into view.

EXPERT'S CIRCLE

Look at a world map and find the lines north and south of the Equator that are labeled Tropic of Cancer and Tropic of Capricorn. Those imaginary lines show the places where the sun is directly overhead on the first day of summer (Cancer) and winter (Capricorn). When these locations on Earth's surface were identified some 2,000 years ago, the sun appeared in the sections of the sky where these constellations were located. Shifts in Earth's rotation have put the sun "in" other constellations on those days, but the names for the lines remain the same.

LEO THE LION

VITALS Leo the Lion · **MAKEUP** 12 stars · **BEST VIEWED** March and April · **LOCATION** Spring, center of chart · **ALPHA STAR** Regulus · **SIZE** 🤚

Is Leo the Lion the famous Sphinx—part lion, part man—from ancient Egypt? Or did Egyptians design the Sphinx to represent the lionlike collection of stars? Either way, it's hard not to see an awesome beast in this noticeable collection of stars. A backward question mark—the Sickle of Leo asterism—marks the lion's head and the alpha star Regulus forms the front legs. Leo is located in a fairly empty part of the sky, which makes it stand out even more. In Greek mythology, the constellation represents the Nemean lion, a man-eater that Hercules was ordered to kill. Its skin was so tough, though, that Hercules broke many of his weapons trying to pierce it. He ended up using his bare hands to strangle the beast.

NAME GAME

The alpha star (α) Regulus was named by Polish astronomer Copernicus in the 1500s. The name means "little king." Because the star was bright and noticeable, it was thought of as a ruler of the heavens.

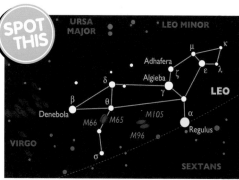

SPOT THIS

URSA MAJOR · LEO MINOR

Adhafera
Algieba
Denebola
LEO
Regulus
VIRGO
SEXTANS

FIND LEO (ABOVE) ON A DIRECT LINE FROM POLARIS, THE NORTH STAR, THROUGH THE OUTER BOWL EDGE OF THE BIG DIPPER.

EXPERT'S CIRCLE

The constellation Leo is rich in deep-sky objects, including the variable star R Leonis and several galaxies. Two of the brightest galaxies are the spiral galaxies M65 and M66 (left), named for their place in Charles Messier's list of sky objects. You can see these galaxies with binoculars and small telescopes.

VIRGO THE VIRGIN

VITALS Virgo the Virgin ◦ **MAKEUP** 13 stars ◦ **BEST VIEWED** May and June ◦ **LOCATION** Spring, southeast quadrant ◦ **ALPHA STAR** Spica ◦ **SIZE** 🖐

Elegant Virgo the Virgin has a human shape, though with wings attached. She also bears a gift: The bright star Spica typically represents a sheaf of wheat that Virgo is carrying. This prominent constellation covers a section of the sky rich in stars and galaxies, such as the Virgo cluster and the Sombrero galaxy. The only woman represented in the zodiac, Virgo has been linked to a number of different goddesses. To ancient Babylonians she was Ishtar, the ruler of family and fertility. The Greeks saw her as Astraea, the goddess of justice, or possibly Demeter, the goddess of agriculture.

SPOT THIS

FROM THE HANDLE OF THE BIG DIPPER, "ARC TO ARCTURUS," FOLLOW A CURVE, AND THEN SPEED SOUTH TO SPICA, THE BRIGHT STAR IN VIRGO (ABOVE).

be a SKYWATCHER!

LOOK FOR THIS! A telescope will reveal a floating hat near the southwestern edge of Virgo—the Sombrero galaxy. The Hubble Space Telescope has captured some very cool images of this awesome shape. Check it out: hubblesite.org/gallery/album/galaxy/pr2003028a/.

TRY THIS!

Virgo has so many galaxies that you need to take some time to look around it. Instead of trying to focus in on specific objects, use a wide-field telescope eyepiece to patiently scan the galaxy fields in the northwestern part of the constellation. A search through the Virgo cluster will show thousands of star clusters and galaxies.

LIBRA THE SCALES

VITALS Libra the Scales ▪ **MAKEUP** 8 stars ▪ **BEST VIEWED** June and July ▪ **LOCATION** Summer, southwest quadrant ▪ **ALPHA STAR** Zubenelgenubi ▪ **SIZE**

The only constellation in the zodiac that doesn't represent a human or animal form, Libra appears between the constellations Scorpius and Virgo. The Scales's stars lack the brightness of their neighbors, but the three brightest ones form a triangle at the top of the shape that is hard to miss. The constellation Libra doesn't have a story of adventure that often explains the constellations associated with humans, gods, or animals. Ancient Greek and Arab astronomers thought of the prominent alpha and beta stars of Libra as the claws of Scorpius the Scorpion. Their names for these stars, Zubenelgenubi and Zubeneschamali, translate as the southern and northern claws. You can see the two stars of binary Zubenelgenubi by using binoculars. Constellation Libra's scales were also associated with the scales held by the Greek goddess of justice or were imagined as being carried by neighboring Virgo.

A LINE FROM THE BRIGHT STAR SPICA IN VIRGO TO ANTARES IN SCORPIUS WILL CUT THE SCALES OF LIBRA (ABOVE) IN HALF.

Did you know?

Even though it isn't very flashy, the constellation Libra was special to the ancient Romans. This might be because the moon was located in Libra when the city of Rome was founded, according to traditional calculations.

be a SKYWATCHER!

LOOK FOR THIS! Delta Librae, a star not far from Libra's main star Zubeneschamali, is an eclipsing variable star. It changes in brightness over a 2.3-day period. Its fast cycle can be seen with the naked eye.

SCORPIUS THE SCORPION

VITALS Scorpius the Scorpion · **MAKEUP** 17 stars · **BEST VIEWED** July and August · **LOCATION** Summer, southwest quadrant · **ALPHA STAR** Antares · **SIZE** 🖐

The shape of the constellation Scorpius the Scorpion matches its namesake animal. Two of its stars rank among the 25 brightest in the sky—Antares and Shaula. The head of the scorpion is located above Antares, which the Romans called Cor Scorpions, or "heart of the scorpion." At the other end, the bright star Shaula represents the scorpion's stinger. Scorpius represents the poisonous animal in Greek mythology that stung and killed the great hunter Orion. The scorpion may have been sent to do its deadly deed by the goddess Artemis, also a hunter. As a result, the two constellations Scorpius and Orion appear on opposite sides of the sky to keep them separated.

SPOT THIS

FIND SCORPIUS (ABOVE) BY LOCATING THE REDDISH BRIGHT STAR ANTARES AT ITS CENTER. LOOK TO THE WEST OF THE TEAPOT SHAPE IN SAGITTARIUS.

Did you know?

Antares is a red supergiant star. Its name means "rival of Mars" and it measures about 300 times larger than the sun.

be a SKYWATCHER!

LOOK FOR THIS! Use Scorpius as a starting point to hunt for nearby star clusters like this one inside Scorpius. Don't miss the Butterfly cluster (M6 on map) near the scorpion's tail that is visible to the naked eye, although binoculars will reveal its distinct butterfly shape. Also nearby is the Ptolemy cluster (M7). It can be seen with the naked eye, but binoculars will offer a better view. Finally, Scorpius X-1 was the first x-ray source discovered after the sun and can be seen only with advanced telescopes.

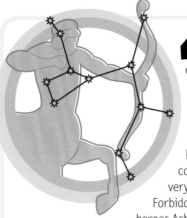

SAGITTARIUS THE ARCHER

VITALS **Sagittarius the Archer** ◦ MAKEUP **22 stars** ◦ BEST VIEWED **March and April** ◦ LOCATION **Summer, southeast quadrant** ◦ ALPHA STAR **Rukbat** ◦ SIZE

Sagittarius the Archer takes the form of a half-man, half-horse centaur holding a bow and arrow. Centaurs are considered brave and strong—and also very wise. (Think of those centaurs in the Forbidden Forest in *Harry Potter*!) The Greek heroes Achilles and Hercules were tutored by a centaur named Chiron, who is often linked to Sagittarius. Sagittarius may also represent an archer racing across the sky to hunt Scorpius the Scorpion. Sagittarius is a large constellation that gives starwatchers a view into the center of the Milky Way. The constellation contains two asterisms, or star patterns, that are a great help in locating it. The famous Teapot asterism forms the core of the centaur's body and shoulders. Connected to the Teapot and pointing to the east is the Milk Dipper asterism. Think of it as scooping milk from the Milky Way.

FIND SAGITTARIUS (ABOVE) BY LOOKING FOR THE TEAPOT ASTERISM IN THE MIDDLE OF THE MILKY WAY. NEXT TO IT YOU'LL FIND THE MILK DIPPER ASTERISM.

Did you know?

Instead of a teapot, ancient Arab astronomers saw the central stars of Sagittarius as a group of ostriches drinking from the Milky Way.

be a SKYWATCHER!

LOOK FOR THIS! Peer into the heart of the Milky Way with binoculars and just above the Teapot asterism you will see the Great Sagittarius Star Cloud. To the right of the cloud, you can view M8, the Lagoon Nebula (large cluster at right), which is also visible to the naked eye under good conditions.

CAPRICORNUS THE SEA GOAT

VITALS Capricornus the Sea Goat · **MAKEUP** 12 stars · **BEST VIEWED** August and September · **LOCATION** Summer, southeast quadrant · **ALPHA STAR** Algedi · **SIZE**

The constellation Capricornus was identified as a goat thousands of years ago. The name of its alpha star, Algedi, is Arabic for "goat." At some later time the constellation was given a fish tail. In one myth, the god Pan—who was a part-human, part-goat satyr, or woodland god—leaped into the Nile River to escape a monster and became part fish. In another tale, the animal represents one of Zeus's warriors who discovered conch shells and the ability to make a deep call when blowing into one. The call frightened away the enemy Titans, so Zeus honored the warrior by placing him in the sky with horns and a fish tail to represent the discovery of the conch shells. Alpha star Algedi appears to the naked eye as an optical binary star, but the two closely aligned stars are actually 500 light-years apart.

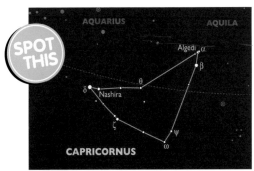

LOCATE CAPRICORNUS (ABOVE) JUST BELOW AND TO THE LEFT OF ALTAIR, THE BRIGHTEST STAR IN THE CONSTELLATION AQUILA AND PART OF THE SUMMER TRIANGLE ASTERISM.

Did you know?

Capricornus is associated with the start of winter because when the idea of the zodiac was created, the sun appeared to be in the area of that constellation during the winter solstice in December. But the Earth's tilted axis produces a wobble when the planet rotates that causes the sun to change location in relation to the constellations over time.

EXPERT'S CIRCLE

In most constellations, stars are labeled according to their apparent magnitude, or brightness, as we view it from Earth. Alpha stars are brightest, followed by beta, and so on, using the Greek alphabet. Capricornus is an exception. Algedi, the alpha star near the "horns" of Capricornus, is actually pretty dim, only the third brightest in the constellation, but it gets a boost from being an optical binary star.

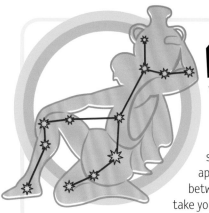

AQUARIUS THE WATER BEARER

VITALS **Aquarius the Water Bearer** · MAKEUP **13 stars** · BEST VIEWED **September and October** · LOCATION **Autumn, southwest quadrant** · ALPHA STAR **Sadalmelik** · SIZE

Aquarius covers a lot of the sky. It stretches out along the ecliptic, the apparent path of the sun across the sky, between Pisces and Capricornus. You can take your pick from a number of myths about the Water Bearer. Does he flood the Nile River to produce healthy crops? Is he filling the great celestial river Eridanus, also a constellation? Or is he pouring the water of life onto Earth? To the ancient Greeks, Aquarius was Zeus's cupbearer, Ganymede. Aquarius is one of the fainter zodiac constellations, located south of the Great Square of Pegasus. It occurs in a very dark region of the sky that ancient astronomers saw as the deep sea, so they gave constellations there "watery" names. Locating Aquarius takes a bit of patience.

NAME GAME

In the desert lands of the ancient Arab world, water brought life to the land and people. It was thought of as good fortune. Perhaps this led Arab astronomers to give the stars of Aquarius names associated with good luck. The alpha star Sadalmelik means "lucky one of the king."

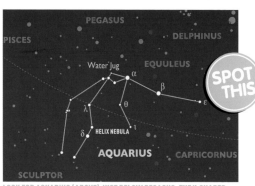

LOOK FOR AQUARIUS (ABOVE) JUST BELOW PEGASUS. THE Y-SHAPED WATER JUG ASTERISM IS THE CONSTELLATION'S MOST OBVIOUS FEATURE.

be a SKYWATCHER!

LOOK FOR THIS! The Helix Nebula in the southern part of Aquarius is one of the closest planetary nebulae to Earth. You can see it as a round, hazy smudge through binoculars and in more detail through a telescope.

PISCES THE FISH

VITALS Pisces the Fish · MAKEUP 17 stars · BEST VIEWED October and November · LOCATION Autumn, southeast quadrant · ALPHA STAR Alrisha · SIZE

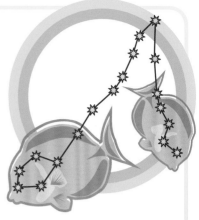

The two actual fish of Pisces are small, but they're held together by a long cord of stars, giving the constellation a wide piece of the sky. All the stars together make a giant V shape. At the southern end of Pisces, the larger fish is represented by a circular shape known as the Circlet asterism. In Greek myth, the goddess Aphrodite and her son Eros changed themselves into fish so they could swim away and escape the sea monster Typhon. To be sure they wouldn't be separated, they bound their tails together with a cord. The cord meets at the constellation's alpha star, Alrisha.

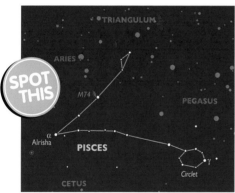

THE LARGER FISH OF PISCES, WITH ITS CIRCLET ASTERISM (ABOVE), SWIMS RIGHT BENEATH THE GREAT SQUARE OF PEGASUS.

be a SKYWATCHER!

LOOK FOR THIS! M74 is a spiral galaxy that gives viewers on Earth a full view of its shape. It contains about 100 billion stars, but overall the galaxy is dim. You can find it with an eight-inch (20-cm) telescope if you have expert help, or see it like this (below) on the Hubble website.

Did you know?

Researchers often look for historical events that may match events described in religious books like the Bible. A rare set of conjunctions—when sky objects appear together—occurred in Pisces in 7 B.C., when Jupiter and Saturn seemed to approach each other three times in one year. They would have looked like a single, very bright star. This might explain the glowing star of Bethlehem seen by shepherds when Christ was born.

Spectacular Sky :
Pleiades

Worldwide tales

The Pleiades have appeared in stories and awed the world for thousands of years. A Native American tale portrays them as lost sisters chased by a bear. The Aztec of Mexico organized their calendar around the Pleiades. And the Celts of Europe used the stars to mark a holiday between autumn and winter that eventually became Halloween.

Like the full moon or the planet Venus at its most brilliant, the bright, jewel-like stars of the Pleiades stand out in the fall and winter skies. Cultures around the world have given them special importance. Though the name refers to a cluster that contains hundreds of stars, it is most commonly known for the seven individual stars known as the Seven Sisters. The Pleiades are "young" stars—only 100 million years old!

Viewing the Pleiades

The Pleiades are best seen as fall moves into winter, with Orion still chasing them in the sky. Orion's belt points to the Pleiades to the northwest.

Seven Sisters

The Seven Sisters are the brightest stars in the cluster. Located in the constellation Taurus, they represent the seven daughters of the Titan Atlas. Annoyed that Orion kept bothering them, they asked Zeus for help. Zeus turned them into doves and later stars, and set them in the sky. Six of the sisters are almost always visible to the naked eye. The seventh will appear if viewing conditions are good. Use binoculars to see the full beauty of this star cluster.

More Amazing Constellations!

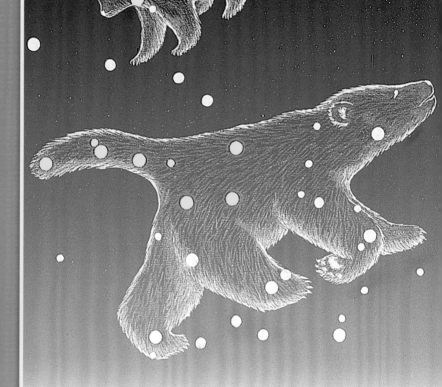

The yellow stars mark the Little Dipper in the constellation Ursa Minor (at top) and the Big Dipper in Ursa Major (at bottom).

In the second century, the ancient Greek astronomer Ptolemy made a list of 48 constellations. Some came from his own observations of the sky. Some came from ancient sky records dating back to Babylonia in the eighth century B.C. They included constellations in the northern sky, such as Hercules and Ursa Major and Ursa Minor (opposite); constellations in the southern sky; and all 12 zodiac constellations.

Travelers under the northern sky looked to Ptolemy's Ursa Minor (Little Bear) to find their way, using the bright star Polaris, or the North Star, at the tip of its tail as a guide.

Since then 40 more constellations have been added, especially as the southern sky became known from voyages in southern oceans. Polynesian navigators used the Southern Cross, the main asterism in the southern sky, as one guide. They'd memorize where it rose above the horizon in morning or set in the evening to determine their location as they sailed across the ocean.

Some of the more recently named constellations have just a few stars and were created to fill in holes in the star map. Some are names of creatures discovered by Dutch navigators in the 16th century, such as the Chamaeleon, or Chameleon. Many of them have names related to tools of science, such as the Telescopium, or Telescope, named by a French astronomer, Nicolas-Louis de Lacaille, in the 18th century.

There are 88 official constellations in all, each with its own star shape and many with stories that ancient peoples in different parts of the world made up to explain what they saw.

Many come from Greek or Roman myth. For instance, Ptolemy's constellation Hercules (the Superhero) is based on the story of the Greek god Zeus's half son, Hercules. The tenth-century Persian astronomer Al-Sufi updated Ptolemy's list to include the names and stories of constellations used by the Arab desert people called the Bedouin. Other stories come from people of early America, West Africa, and China.

The following pages describe 41 key constellations that people who live north of the Equator would see in some places at least part of the year.

You'll discover which seasonal sky chart on pages 68 through 85 will help you locate the constellation at the best time of year. Check the charts often as you read the entries. Remember that although a certain constellation might be listed as best viewed in spring, summer, autumn, or winter, you can still see it at other times of the year!

ANDROMEDA THE CHAINED MAIDEN

VITALS Andromeda the Chained Maiden · **MAKEUP** 16 stars · **BEST VIEWED** October and November · **LOCATION** Autumn, center of chart · **ALPHA STAR** Alpheratz · **SIZE** 〰

The stars of Andromeda, though dim, are easy to find and its story is key to understanding the constellations around it. In Greek myth, Andromeda stars in a family drama that involves the characters of five other nearby constellations: Cassiopeia, Perseus, Cetus, Cepheus, and Pegasus. Queen Cassiopeia of Ethiopia boasted that her daughter Andromeda was more beautiful than daughters of the sea god Nereus. The boast angered the great sea god Poseidon, who took revenge by sending Cetus the sea monster to destroy the kingdom. Cassiopeia and her husband, King Cepheus, offered to sacrifice their daughter, Andromeda, and chained her to a rock in order to save the kingdom. At the last moment, Perseus arrived on his winged horse, Pegasus, and saved her. The constellation contains the Andromeda galaxy (M31). It's a spiral galaxy similar to our own Milky Way and is visible to the naked eye.

Did you know?

It's uncommon for constellations to share a star, but Alpheratz is both the brightest star in Andromeda and part of the Great Square of Pegasus.

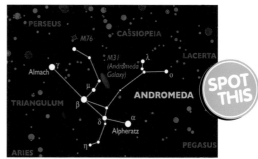

SPOT THIS

LOCATE ANDROMEDA (ABOVE) UNDER CASSIOPEIA'S W AND JUST NORTHEAST OF THE GREAT SQUARE OF PEGASUS.

be a SKYWATCHER!

LOOK FOR THIS! Andromeda is a constellation worth getting to know. In addition to the Andromeda galaxy, it includes the quirky Mira variable star, R Andromedae, which shifts in brightness by eight magnitudes, or levels of brightness. Scientists have discovered that it contains an element named technetium, which is rarely found on Earth.

ANTLIA THE AIR PUMP

VITALS Antlia the Air Pump • **MAKEUP** 3 stars
• **BEST VIEWED** March and April • **LOCATION** Spring, southwest
quadrant • **ALPHA STAR** Alpha Antliae • **SIZE** 🖐

Like many other southern constellations, Antlia represents a scientific device. In the 18th century, French astronomer Nicolas-Louis de Lacaille discovered the constellation Antlia, which means "the pump," from his viewing point at the Cape of Good Hope in South Africa. He named it for the air pump that had been developed about a century earlier that allowed scientists to study the properties of vacuums, spaces from which air has been removed. Antlia is visible in northern skies for at least part of the year. It contains the galaxy NGC 2997, which can be seen faintly through a small telescope. It also includes two binary stars. One of them can be seen as two separate stars with good binoculars.

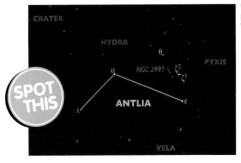

WITH A CLEAR VIEW OF THE SOUTHERN HORIZON, LOCATE ANTLIA (ABOVE) FIVE FIST-WIDTHS BELOW REGULUS IN LEO.

Did you know?

Lacaille, who also observed and named the southern constellations Telescopium and Microscopium, along with ten others, noted over 10,000 southern sky stars during his trip south of the Equator.

TRY THIS!

Here's a really easy experiment! To see why scientists are interested in air pressure and gas, blow up a balloon and then simply let it go. It should fly around a bit, showing the power of a gas under pressure. Your lungs pushed air (a gas) into the balloon, creating pressure inside it. (Be sure to dispose of the balloon properly. Balloons can harm wildlife.)

AQUILA THE EAGLE

VITALS Aquila the Eagle · **MAKEUP 12 stars** · **BEST VIEWED August and September** · **LOCATION Summer, southeast quadrant** · **ALPHA STAR Altair** · **SIZE** 🤚

Aquila the Eagle flies through the star fields of the Milky Way with outstretched wings. The pattern of this constellation's stars makes it easy for a skywatcher to imagine a bird, although sometimes drawings of the pattern show the eagle flying off in different directions. No matter which way you look at it, this is a very birdlike group of stars—and Aquila's alpha star, Altair, makes a very fine head. The name Altair even means "eagle" in Arabic. Altair is one of the brightest stars in the sky and a very good reference point for locating the constellation Aquila. Altair forms part of the Summer Triangle asterism along with Vega in constellation Lyra and Deneb in Cygnus. The constellation Aquila was named by ancient stargazers in Mesopotamia (today's Iraq), and the image of the bird stuck. In later Greek myth, the eagle was the companion of the chief god, Zeus, and carried the mighty god's thunderbolts for him. Aquila is also thought to have carried the young shepherd Ganymede to the sky to serve as Zeus's cupbearer. We know Ganymede through the myth that explains the nearby zodiac constellation Aquarius.

SPOT THIS

THE BRIGHT STAR ALTAIR (ABOVE), PART OF THE SUMMER TRIANGLE, MARKS THE EAGLE'S HEAD. READ ABOUT THE SUMMER TRIANGLE ON PAGES 80–81.

Did you know?

Aquila lies close enough to Earth's Equator to be seen from just about any place on Earth.

be a SKYWATCHER!

LOOK FOR THIS! Aquila contains the variable star Eta Aquilae. It is one of the faster Cepheid variable stars, stars that change brightness regularly. Eta Aquilae changes its brightness every week!

AURIGA THE CHARIOTEER

VITALS **Auriga the Charioteer** ▪ **MAKEUP** 7 stars
▪ **BEST VIEWED December and January** ▪ **LOCATION Winter,**
center of chart ▪ **ALPHA STAR Capella** ▪ **SIZE**

Auriga the Charioteer drives his
chariot down the middle of the Milky
Way. The constellation lies along the
galactic equator, the great imaginary
circle that passes through the densest
part of the Milky Way. Auriga's bright star,
Capella, helps skywatchers locate the constellation, although it takes a bit of imagination to turn
this squarish group of stars into a charioteer. Auriga has several
connections to Greek mythology. One involves Hephaestus, the
disabled blacksmith god, whose damaged legs inspired him to build a
chariot so he could travel. The other includes his son, Erichthonius. He
was a mythical king of Athens who received special training from the
goddess Athena. She showed him how to harness four horses to his
chariot. The Greek astronomer Ptolemy included Auriga on his list of
48 constellations in the second century.

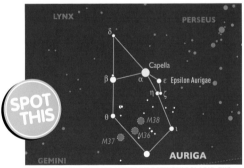

AURIGA IS FOUND ON A STRAIGHT LINE BETWEEN POLARIS, THE
NORTH STAR, AND ORION. ITS BRIGHT STAR, CAPELLA, STANDS OUT.

Did you know?

Southwest of the star Capella
lies the star Epsilon Aurigae (ε).
It is called an eclipsing variable
star. That means it is a binary
star whose brightness depends
on the location of the partner
star that orbits around it. When
the partner star eclipses Capella
by moving in front of it, Capella
grows dimmer.

be a SKYWATCHER!

**LOOK FOR THIS! Sitting in the middle of the Milky Way, Auriga
is rich in star clusters (right) that can be seen with binoculars.
The one labeled M37 on star maps is really dense with stars.**

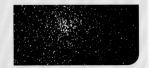

BOÖTES THE HERDSMAN

VITALS Boötes the Herdsman ▪ **MAKEUP** 13 stars ▪ **BEST VIEWED** June ▪ **LOCATION** Summer, center of chart ▪ **ALPHA STAR** Arcturus ▪ **SIZE** 🤚

Boötes the Herdsman is a famous constellation in the summer sky. It's also easy to find, thanks to its shape and the bright alpha star Arcturus that forms one of the Herdsman's knees. Arcturus is easy to find because it lies on a curve from the handle of the Big Dipper. Stargazers today often think that Boötes looks like a kite, and even has a tail to help it soar. But in Greek, Boötes means "plowman" or "herdsman." This figure does not appear to be a typical herder because in some versions of his myth he is herding the bears of the nearby constellations Ursa Major and Ursa Minor. Arcturus is a name of Greek origin that means "bear keeper." Other Greek tales make Boötes the son of Callisto, who was changed into a bear by Zeus's angry wife. Some tales say he is Plotous, the son of Demeter, goddess of the harvest. The nearby dogs of Canes Venatici may be Boötes's companions.

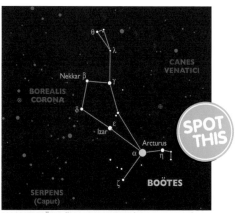

TO LOCATE BOÖTES, "ARC TO ARCTURUS" (FOLLOW A CURVE) FROM THE HANDLE OF THE BIG DIPPER TO THE FIRST BRIGHT STAR.

NAME GAME

How do you pronounce the name of this constellation? Boo-teez or Bo-o-teez? The mark over the second *o* is a clue to pronunciation. It means that the *o* is pronounced. So it's Bo-o-teez.

be a SKYWATCHER!

LOOK FOR THIS! January's Quadrantid meteor shower originates in a region of the sky that includes Boötes, Hercules, and Draco.

CAMELOPARDALIS THE GIRAFFE

VITALS Camelopardalis the Giraffe · **MAKEUP 9 stars**
· **BEST VIEWED December and January** · **LOCATION Northeast quadrant**
· **ALPHA STAR Alpha Camelopardalis** · **SIZE** 🖐

Is it a camel? A leopard? A giraffe? This
small modern constellation fills a gap
in the sky between the bears—Ursa
Major and Ursa Minor—and Perseus.
It was described in 1613 by the Dutch
astronomer Petrus Plancius. Plancius saw
the constellation as a giraffe and gave it the
name Camelopardalis, which comes from the Greek
word for the long-necked animal. Though it seems pretty funny today,
the ancient Greeks thought the giraffe was a cross between the camel
and the leopard. It combined the long face and lumpy back of a camel
with the spots of a leopard. Other stories linked the constellation to
the camel in the Bible that carried Rebecca to her marriage with Isaac.
Camelopardalis trots high in the northern sky, a neighbor of Polaris,
the North Star. It stays visible throughout the year in the Northern
Hemisphere, but it's a faint constellation. If you find it, try to spot
the star cluster NGC 1502, visible through a telescope.

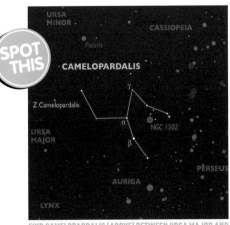

FIND CAMELOPARDALIS (ABOVE) BETWEEN URSA MAJOR AND
PERSEUS, SOUTH OF POLARIS.

Did you know?

Z Camelopardalis (left and below)
is one of the five key stars in Camelopardalis. It's called a cataclysmic
variable star. It becomes super
bright, and then decreases. Every 27
years this star is covered by a companion star in an eclipse. Its period
of darkness can last for two years!

CANES VENATICI THE HUNTING DOGS

VITALS Canes Venatici the Hunting Dogs • **MAKEUP** 2 stars • **BEST VIEWED** May and June • **LOCATION** Spring, center of chart • **ALPHA STAR** Cor Caroli • **SIZE** ✋

It's only two stars, but somehow the Polish astronomer Johannes Hevelius decided that the stars would be dogs when he was working on the creation of a new constellation. The Hunting Dogs appear where you might expect to find two leashed hounds in relation to the constellation of Boötes the Herdsman—running to the west of him. Another way to think about these dogs is to imagine them running between the legs of Ursa Major, the big bear that the dogs are chasing. These two northern stars became one of the 88 official constellations in the 17th century. The main star of Canes Venatici is called Cor Caroli, which is Latin for "heart of Charles." The story goes that the famous English astronomer Edmond Halley named the star in honor of King Charles II.

CANES VENATICI

YOU WILL FIND CANES VENATICI IN SPRING BELOW—AND PARALLEL TO—THE HANDLE OF THE BIG DIPPER IN THE CONSTELLATION URSA MAJOR (SEE THE SPRING SKY CHART ON PAGES 74–75).

be a SKYWATCHER!

LOOK FOR THIS! The Whirlpool galaxy (M51), seen here in an image from the Hubble Space Telescope, can also be viewed with a six-inch (15-cm) telescope by looking in the sky neighborhood between Canes Venatici and Ursa Major.

Did you know?

In the second century, Greek astronomer Ptolemy included the stars of Canes Venatici in his work, but he did not put them in any constellation—leaving them up for grabs for later astronomers!

CANIS MAJOR THE LARGER DOG

VITALS Canis Major the Larger Dog · **MAKEUP** 13 stars
· **BEST VIEWED** January and February · **LOCATION** Southeast quadrant ·
ALPHA STAR Sirius · **SIZE**

Canis Major is a skywatching newbie's dream. It has the superbright star Sirius, an interesting story, and a shape that's easy to imagine—and locate. Orion's belt points directly to Sirius, the chest of the Larger Dog. From its pointy nose to the tip of its tail, this collection of stars clearly outlines a dog. In mythology, Canis Major is Orion's hunting dog, along with the smaller Canis Minor. They chase down nearby Lepus the Hare. In another story, Canis Major earns a place in the sky by beating a fox in a race. Along with its smaller dog companion, Canis Major also may be waiting for scraps under the table of the Gemini twins.

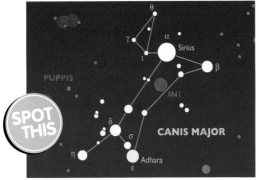

LOOK SOUTHEAST FROM ORION'S BELT TO SPOT SIRIUS, THE SKY'S BRIGHTEST STAR, WHICH IS THE "CHEST" OF CANIS MAJOR (ABOVE).

Did you know?

Have you ever heard someone mention the "dog days of summer" when it's hot and sticky? The dog in the saying is the Dog Star, Sirius, which rises alongside the sun in summer. People once believed the two stars together brought extra heat to the Earth. But Sirius is too far away for its heat to affect our climate.

EXPERT'S CIRCLE

Outshone by Sirius, the superdense white dwarf star Sirius B, aka the Pup, is just below Sirius, but too tiny to label on the chart above. Sirius B was discovered in 1862 when a new large telescope was pointed at Sirius. The dwarf star is normally hard to see, but in 2022 it will move far enough away from Sirius for skywatchers to get a better look.

CANIS MINOR THE SMALLER DOG

VITALS Canis Minor the Smaller Dog ▪ **MAKEUP 2 stars**
▪ **BEST VIEWED January and February** ▪ **LOCATION Winter, southeast
quadrant** ▪ **ALPHA STAR Procyon** ▪ **SIZE** 👍

For a small constellation, Canis Minor owns a rich set of stories. One story makes him Orion's smaller hunting dog. Another puts Canis Minor under the table of Castor and Pollux, the Gemini twins, waiting for scraps. And yet another makes him Helen of Troy's favorite pup that allowed her to elope with the Trojan prince Paris. Together with Betelgeuse in Orion and Canis Major's Sirius, Canis Minor's alpha star, Procyon, forms the Winter Triangle. This asterism helps orient winter stargazers. Originally, Procyon was the only star included in Canis Minor. Then a second star was added. Procyon lies only 11.2 light-years from Earth and is the eighth brightest star in the night sky. Despite the flashy appearance of Procyon, this constellation lacks any brightly shining deep-sky objects.

Laugh Out Loud!

What should you do if you see a green alien from another planet?

A. Wait until it's ripe!

Did you know?

It's good to keep an eye on the sky: An astronomer studying one December meteor shower in 1964 ended up discovering another. The new one he saw was streaming from the neighborhood of Canis Minor and is now known as the Canis Minorid shower.

NORTHEAST OF THE LARGER DOG, CANIS MAJOR, LOOK FOR CANIS MINOR'S MAIN STAR, PROCYON (ABOVE).

CEPHEUS THE KING

VITALS **Cepheus the King** • MAKEUP **10 stars**
• BEST VIEWED **September and October** • LOCATION **Autumn, center of chart** • ALPHA STAR **Alderamin** • SIZE 🤚

Cepheus is a high northern constellation, visible all year long from places in the Northern Hemisphere as it circles the celestial north pole. The stars of this constellation are not bright, but the main ones make a fairly distinct house shape in a pretty empty part of the sky. The story of Cepheus is intertwined with that of other nearby constellations linked to the drama that involved Andromeda. As the husband of Queen Cassiopeia, who boasted about their daughter Andromeda's beauty, Cepheus is more of a bystander in the story. To calm a wrathful Poseidon, Cassiopeia and Cepheus had Andromeda chained to a rock as bait for the sea monster Cetus. But Perseus came to save the day, and Andromeda was released. Look for a reddish "garnet star" near the king's feet, known as Mu Cephei.

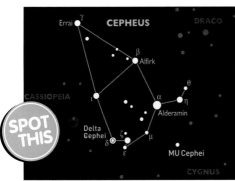

A TRIANGLE OF THREE STARS FORMS THE UPPER BODY OF CEPHEUS (ABOVE). THE TOP STAR, ERRAI, POINTS TOWARD POLARIS, THE NORTH STAR. CEPHEUS LIES TO THE RIGHT OF THE OPEN SIDE OF CASSIOPEIA.

Did you know?

Cepheus lends its name to Cepheid variable stars. These kinds of stars change in brightness over a regular period of time.

be a SKYWATCHER!

LOOK FOR THIS! The star Delta Cephei, just above the constellation Lacerta near one of the king's feet, shifts in brightness every 5.5 days. The regular changes have helped astronomers understand variable stars and determine how far away those stars are from Earth.

DELTA CEPHEI

CETUS THE SEA MONSTER

VITALS Cetus the Sea Monster · **MAKEUP 14 stars**
· **BEST VIEWED November** · **LOCATION Autumn, southeast quadrant**
· **ALPHA STAR Menkar** · **SIZE**

The sea monster Cetus is a whale-shaped constellation covering a wide expanse of the sky. So if you're "fishing" for Cetus in the Heavenly Waters group of constellations, be sure to choose a clear, dark night to have a good chance of spotting it. Cetus has ties to myth and maybe real life, something unusual for many constellations. A 40-foot (12-m) skeleton, perhaps of a whale, that was brought to ancient Rome might have been a model for this constellation. You'll find Cetus along with other water-based constellations such as Aquarius and Eridanus. Cetus has a big role in the myth of Andromeda as the sea monster Poseidon sent to punish Ethiopia for Queen Cassiopeia's boasting. Cetus may also be connected to the Bible story of Jonah, who was swallowed by a whale.

Did you know?

Mira (right, on map) is an old star. In 2007, scientists discovered that it has a comet-like tail several light-years long. This is the material the star is losing as it dies.

SPOT THIS

CETUS (ABOVE) LIES BETWEEN THE CONSTELLATION PISCES AND TAURUS. ITS 14 STARS FORM A CONNECTED HEAD AND TAIL.

EXPERT'S CIRCLE

Though it's often referred to as a sea monster, Cetus is more likely a whale. Its name was lent to the order of mammals known as Cetacea, which includes whales, dolphins, and porpoises.

COLUMBA THE DOVE

VITALS Columba the Dove • **MAKEUP 7 stars**
• **BEST VIEWED January and February** • **LOCATION Winter, southeast quadrant** • **ALPHA STAR Phact** • **SIZE**

The tiny dove Columba flies in a crowded neighborhood of the sky. Its stars compete for attention with superstars Sirius and Canopus. These bright stars actually act as guideposts to finding Columba. You'll have a better chance of spotting it if you make sure you have the best viewing conditions. Columba is a modern constellation, created in the 16th century by Dutch astronomer Petrus Plancius. It celebrates a dove that played a big part in the biblical story of Noah's ark. The dove was released from the ark as a kind of scout after the rains had stopped. When the bird returned with an olive branch in its bill, it was taken as a sign that land was near and the floodwaters were receding. Plancius chose well when he put the dove in the Heavenly Waters neighborhood of the sky.

THE MAIN STARS OF COLUMBA (ABOVE) LOOK LIKE THREE ARMS OR LEGS SPIRALING FROM A MEDIUM-BRIGHT STAR AT THE CENTER.

Did you know?

Using a map of the southern stars that a ship's pilot had created for him, Plancius was the first to fill out the emptier southern sky map with constellations.

Laugh Out Loud!

What did the alien cook for lunch?

A. Unidentified frying objects!

COMA BERENICES THE HAIR OF BERENICES

VITALS Coma Berenices the Hair of Berenices · **MAKEUP** 3 stars · **BEST VIEWED** May and June · **LOCATION** Spring, southeast quadrant · **ALPHA STAR** Alpha Coma Berenices · **SIZE**

Coma Berenices formed part of other constellations—a wisp of Virgo's hair or the tuft of Leo's tail—until the 16th-century Danish astronomer Tycho Brahe helped make it a constellation in its own right. Coma Berenices means "hair of Berenice" in Latin, and it's the only constellation to represent a real person. Berenice was an Egyptian queen, the wife of Ptolemy III. As Ptolemy marched off to war, Berenice made a deal with the goddess of love, Aphrodite. She offered her beautiful, flowing hair in return for her husband's safe return. After the wish was granted and Ptolemy was safe at home, the astronomer of the royal court convinced the king and queen that a grateful Aphrodite had placed the queen's gift in the stars.

Laugh Out Loud!

What should you do if you meet an angry alien?

A. Give it some space!

Did you know?

In the middle of Coma Berenices is M64, also known as the Black Eye galaxy. Visible through a small telescope, the spiral galaxy looks like a big bruise, just as the name suggests!

SPOT THIS

LOOK FOR THREE STARS THAT MAKE ALMOST A RIGHT ANGLE JUST NORTH OF THE CLUSTER OF GALAXIES IN VIRGO AND SOUTH OF CANES VENATICI (ABOVE).

CORONA AUSTRALIS THE SOUTHERN CROWN

VITALS Corona Australis the Southern Crown • MAKEUP 5 stars • BEST VIEWED July and August • LOCATION Summer, southeast quadrant • ALPHA STAR Alpha Coronae Australis • SIZE (͡)

There's not much bling in Corona Australis, the Southern Crown. This dim constellation will be invisible to many skywatchers in the Northern Hemisphere because it never gets very far above the horizon. It is mostly a southern constellation, climbing just high enough into the northern sky for part of the year that the ancient Greek astronomer Ptolemy was able to include it in his original charts of the sky. While it's not very showy, Corona Australis has a rich mythology. Many of those myths refer to a crown made of laurel or fig leaves, a common way of showing honor or respect to a person in ancient times. One version makes Corona Australis the crown of Centaurus the Centaur. Another has Apollo fashion the crown from the leaves of his love, Daphne, who had been transformed into a laurel tree. The constellation is home to an active star-forming region composed of the Coronet cluster and the Corona Australis Nebula. Only advanced deep-sky tele-scopes can view that region, which boasts about 30 infant stars.

THE CONSTELLATION'S FIVE KEY STARS (ABOVE), VISIBLE MAINLY IN THE SOUTHERN SKY, CAN BE FOUND AT THE FEET OF SAGITTARIUS AND JUST WEST OF THE BRIGHT TAIL STAR IN SCORPIUS.

SPOT THIS

Did you know?

Ancient Chinese astronomers saw Corona Australis as a large turtle with a domed shell that sat on a riverbank in the sky.

Spectacular Sky: Andromeda Galaxy

Galaxies are one of the basic building blocks of the universe. They are areas with enough gases, space dust, and other matter for stars to form—and enough gravity to hold everything together. We now know that the Milky Way, Earth's home galaxy, is only one of billions of galaxies in the universe. The galaxy closest to us is the Andromeda galaxy, a spiral galaxy "only" 2.5 million light-years away. It is located between the constellations Cassiopeia and Andromeda and is visible on a dark night as a smudge in the sky. The light we see from Andromeda left the galaxy several million years ago, when our human ancestors were hunting on the plains of Africa! Astronomers in the tenth century took note of a "little cloud" that we now know is a separate galaxy that will eventually collide with our Milky Way some four billion years from now.

Andromeda galaxy

Edwin Hubble

In the 1920s, Edwin Hubble—the astron-omer for whom the Hubble Space Tele-scope (above) is named—used the most powerful telescope in the world to study the "little cloud." He figured out that the object was too far away to be part of the Milky Way and was, in fact, a separate galaxy, the Andromeda. It was the first proof that other galaxies existed.

Andromeda constellation

The Andromeda galaxy got its name from the nearby constellation Andromeda (right). On star charts the galaxy is labeled as M31. Look for a stretched-out patch of light on a line from the lowest part of Cassiopeia to the middle of the constellation Andromeda. You can see the galaxy with the naked eye. Binoculars reveal its spiral form.

CORONA BOREALIS THE NORTHERN CROWN

VITALS Corona Borealis the Northern Crown • MAKEUP 7 stars • BEST VIEWED June and July • LOCATION Summer, center of chart • ALPHA STAR Alphecca • SIZE 🖐

In ancient Greece, Dionysus was the god of fun. He liked nothing more than to throw a big party with wine, music, and some silly behavior. So it's not a surprise that his crown ended up in the sky in the form of the constellation Northern Crown, Corona Borealis. According to Greek mythology, Dionysus had asked the princess of Crete, Ariadne, to marry him. She was not very impressed, though, because she thought he was a mere mortal. To win her love, Dionysus threw his crown into the sky, where it stuck, proving that he was a god. The crown toss changed Ariadne's mind and they married. In American Indian lore, the seven distinct stars of the constellation represent a semicircle of tents. Some stars in Corona Borealis vary significantly in brightness. Three stars—Epsilon (ε), Kappa (κ), and Omicron (o, which is too faint to plot)—may have at least one planet orbiting each of them.

Did you know?

The star T Coronae Borealis, just outside the main constellation, is a variable star caused by a nova explosion. It's not usually visible to the naked eye, but it became one of the brightest stars in the constellation in 1866 and again in 1946.

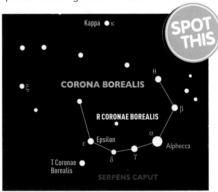

LOOK FOR AN OBVIOUS SEMICIRCLE OF SEVEN STARS, SQUEEZED IN BETWEEN THE BIGGER, BRIGHTER NEIGHBORS BOÖTES AND HERCULES. CORONA BOREALIS LIES JUST NORTH OF THE HEAD OF SERPENS, CALLED SERPENS CAPUT (ABOVE).

R CORONAE BOREALIS

EXPERT'S CIRCLE

The strange star R Coronae Borealis would normally be called a nova. But it occasionally disappears or becomes dim after dark material erupts from its surface, so it's been called a "reverse nova."

CORVUS THE CROW

VITALS **Corvus the Crow** · MAKEUP **5 stars** · BEST VIEWED **April and May**
· LOCATION **Spring, southeast quadrant** · ALPHA STAR **Alchiba**
· SIZE ⟨⟨⟩⟩

In Greek mythology, Corvus the Crow is a pesky bird that angered the god Apollo and ended up banished to the sky as a result. The tale involves the neighboring constellations of Hydra the Sea Serpent and Crater the Cup. Apollo had asked Corvus to fetch him a cup of water, represented by the constellation Crater. The crow got distracted by a tempting fig and stopped to wait for it to ripen so he could eat it. Even though he got the cup, Corvus knew his tardiness would get him in trouble, so he grabbed a serpent (Hydra) and took it back with him. When he got to Apollo, he told the god that he was late because the serpent had attacked him. Apollo could tell Corvus was lying and he tossed him into the sky.

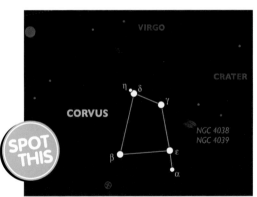

LOOK NEAR HYDRA'S TAIL FOR THE FIVE STARS OF CORVUS, FOUR FOR THE BODY AND ONE FOR THE LEGS.

be a SKYWATCHER!

LOOK FOR THIS! Just outside the stars of Corvus, the Ring-tailed galaxy is visible with an eight-inch (20-cm) telescope. It's actually a pair of galaxies (NGC 4038 and NGC 4039 on the map) in collision with each other!

EXPERT'S CIRCLE

To understand the night sky, it helps to know mythology from ancient Greece and Rome. The figures represented in the stars play roles in a number of epic stories that are often intertwined. Constellations near each other are usually part of the same story. Corvus, for example, is mentioned in some stories about the multiheaded serpent Hydra that Hercules killed.

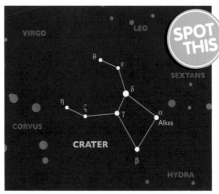

CRATER THE CUP

VITALS Crater the Cup · **MAKEUP** 8 stars · **BEST VIEWED** April and May · **LOCATION** Spring, southeast quadrant · **ALPHA STAR** Alkes · **SIZE** 👆

The eight stars of the constellation Crater make an unmistakable goblet shape. Four stars form the thick base of the goblet and four more form the wide cup, which opens toward the bright star Spica in the constellation Virgo. Crater appears in the spring sky right above the associated constellation Hydra and just west of Corvus, another associated constellation. There have been many stories suggested for the presence of this cup in the night sky. In Greek mythology, Crater represents the vessel brought to Apollo by Corvus, a crow. Apollo tossed both the crow and the cup into the sky, along with Hydra, a sea serpent, when he realized Corvus had lied about the reason he was late bringing a requested cup of water to Apollo. Some sky observers connect the cup to the constellation Aquarius the Water Bearer that occupies the same section of the sky in summer. More recent astronomers associate the cup with the Holy Grail. This was the chalice that Jesus drank from during the Last Supper that medieval knights searched far and wide for. Others see it as the wine goblet of Noah, builder of the biblical ark. The stars in Crater are on the dim side, but Spica in Virgo is a good guide for helping to find its location.

Did you know?

Ancient astronomers considered Crater to be a spike on the back of the sea serpent of the constellation Hydra. But Hydra was such a large and complicated constellation, it was broken into smaller pieces that became their own constellations. The constellation Crater is one of them.

IN THE SPRING SKY, LOOK FOR CRATER'S EIGHT STARS NORTH OF THE CONSTELLATION HYDRA AND WEST OF CORVUS.

CYGNUS THE SWAN

VITALS Cygnus • **MAKEUP 14 STARS** • **BEST VIEWED August and September** • **LOCATION Summer, northeast quadrant** • **ALPHA STAR Deneb** • **SIZE**

Cygnus the Swan soars along the Milky Way on late summer nights, its tail lighted by bright star Deneb. Looking at Cygnus, it is easy to see the outline of a long-necked swan flying overhead. But which swan? Starwatchers can choose from a number of mythological explanations. Cygnus could be Zeus, who transformed into a swan to attract Leda. It could also be Orpheus, who was killed and turned into a swan for rejecting a group of maidens. He was placed into the sky next to his beloved lyre, the musical instrument represented in the constellation Lyra. Cygnus could also be one of the nasty birds that Hercules was ordered to slay as part of his 12 labors. Cygnus's alpha star, Deneb, forms the Summer Triangle along with Altair in Aquila and Vega in Lyra.

THE 14 STARS OF THE SWAN'S WINGS, NECK, AND HEAD (ABOVE) SOAR LIKE A MIGRATING BIRD. LOCATE BRIGHT STAR DENEB IN THE SUMMER TRIANGLE. IT'S THE SWAN'S TAIL.

LOOK FOR THIS! On the sky map near Deneb, look for a bright cloud called the North America Nebula (NGC 7000). The nebula, just behind a patch of bright stars, can be seen with the naked eye under good, dark conditions. The nebula's name comes from its shape!

Did you know?

The constellation Cygnus has helped astronomers clear up several mysteries. Cygnus A was among the first galaxies to be identified by the radio-wave emissions that it gives off. Cygnus X-1, a type of black hole, helped confirm the existence of black holes. Scientists tracked x-rays from a stream of gas that left a star and headed toward an unseen object—the black hole!

DELPHINUS THE DOLPHIN

VITALS Delphinus the Dolphin • **MAKEUP 5 stars** • **BEST VIEWED August through September** • **LOCATION Summer, northeast quadrant** • **ALPHA STAR Sualocin** • **SIZE**

The distinct shape of Delphinus the Dolphin swims overhead in the late summer sky in the area of the sky known as the Heavenly Waters. The constellation contains five dim stars. Four stars form the body and the fifth is the creature's curved tail. The little dolphin holds a place in the sky because he became a favorite of the Greek sea god Poseidon after doing him a big favor. Delphinus was able to convince the sea nymph Amphitrite to marry Poseidon after the god himself had tried and failed to win her attention. The constellation's gamma (γ) star is an optical binary star, best viewed through a telescope. Its dimmer star has a greenish tinge.

Did you know?

The four stars in the body of the dolphin form the asterism called Job's Coffin, named after the biblical character to whom God sent many misfortunes to prove his faith.

LOCATE THE FIVE STARS OF DELPHINUS (ABOVE) JUST WEST OF A STRAIGHT LINE TRACED BETWEEN ALTAIR IN THE CONSTELLATION AQUILA AND DENEB IN THE CONSTELLATION CYGNUS.

DRACO THE DRAGON

VITALS **Draco the Dragon** ▪ MAKEUP **15 stars** ▪ BEST VIEWED **May and June**
▪ LOCATION **Spring, northeast quadrant** ▪ ALPHA STAR **Thuban**
▪ SIZE

Draco the Dragon circles overhead throughout much of the year. It is one of the constellations closest to the celestial north pole, the point in space you would reach if you drew a line straight up from Earth's North Pole. In fact, Draco's brightest star, Thuban, used to be the pole star instead of Polaris. That's because Earth wobbles a little on its axis as it rotates, causing the direction north to change a bit gradually as well. Starting with its tail between Ursa Major and Ursa Minor, Draco skulks along with its head pointing at Hercules. The ancient Greeks believed this constellation represented the dragon Ladon that was one of the many beasts killed by Hercules.

SPOT THIS

FIFTEEN STARS MAKE UP DRACO'S BODY AND TAIL. THE TAIL LIES RIGHT BETWEEN THE LARGER AND SMALLER BEARS, URSA MAJOR AND URSA MINOR.

be a SKYWATCHER!

LOOK FOR THIS! Check out the amazing Cat's Eye Nebula (NGC 6543) in Draco in these images from the Hubble Space Telescope at hubblesite.org/gallery/album/nebula/pr2004027a/.

Did you know?

One of the year's heaviest meteor showers, the Quadrantids erupt from the region of the sky where the constellations Draco, Boötes, and Hercules meet. The Quadrantids occur in the beginning of January and last only a few hours.

EQUULEUS THE LITTLE HORSE

VITALS Equuleus the Little Horse **MAKEUP** 4 stars **BEST VIEWED** July and August **LOCATION** Summer, southeast quadrant **ALPHA STAR** Kitalpha **SIZE** 👍

The second smallest constellation in terms of area, Equuleus appears in a crowded region of the northern sky where it is overshadowed by the larger horse constellation, Pegasus. Its name comes from the Latin for "little horse." Equuleus is thought to represent Celeris, the brother-horse of Pegasus. In Greek mythology, Pegasus is best known as the noble winged steed of Perseus, slayer of Medusa (monster with the snake hairdo) and savior of Andromeda. Celeris belonged to Castor, who along with his brother, Pollux, represents the twins of Gemini. Castor was famed for his skill on horseback and received Celeris as a gift from the messenger god, Hermes. When looking for Equuleus, don't think of an entire horse, just search for four faint stars representing a horse's head and neck.

Laugh Out Loud!

What kind of saddle do you put on a space horse?

A. A saddle-lite!

Did you know?

The alpha star, known as Kitalpha, is the only standout feature of the constellation Little Horse. Think of it as the horse's muzzle. You'll have to imagine its body!

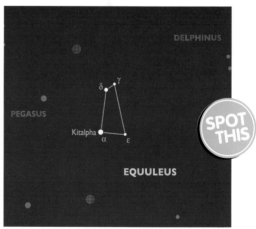

LOOK CAREFULLY FOR EQUULEUS (ABOVE) BETWEEN ITS NEIGHBORS, THE CONSTELLATIONS PEGASUS AND DELPHINUS.

GRUS THE CRANE

VITALS **Grus the Crane** · MAKEUP **12 stars** · BEST VIEWED **September** · LOCATION **Autumn, southwest quadrant** · ALPHA STAR **Alnair** · SIZE 🖐

Until 1603, Grus the Crane was part of the constellation Piscis Austrinus (Southern Fish), German astronomer Johann Bayer set aside this group of stars in honor of the bird that the ancient Egyptians had made the symbol of the astronomer. Grus does look something like a crane, a bird with a long neck, long body, and skinny legs. Over time, the constellation has had other bird names as well, such as the Stork, the Heron, and the Flamingo. Bayer was one of a few astronomers who reworked and named new constellations to fill out the maps of the sky, add southern stars, and break up shapes that were thought to be too large. Grus is mainly a southern constellation that makes a brief appearance in the northern sky in the fall.

TWELVE STARS FORM THE BODY AND WINGS OF GRUS THE CRANE (ABOVE). THEY RISE BRIEFLY ABOVE THE HORIZON IN THE SOUTHWEST SECTION OF THE NORTHERN SKY IN FALL.

Did you know?

Grus contains a group of four spiral galaxies, known as the Grus Quartet, that are pulling each other closer together. Millions of years from now, the four galaxies will likely merge into one.

be a SKYWATCHER!

LOOK FOR THIS! In the center of Grus is an X shape. Three of its stars, including the alpha star Alnair, are brighter than the other stars in the constellation.

ALNAIR

HERCULES THE SUPERHERO

VITALS Hercules the Superhero · **MAKEUP** 21 stars · **BEST VIEWED** July and August · **LOCATION** Summer, center of chart · **ALPHA STAR** Rasalgethi · **SIZE**

One of the giants of the sky, the constellation that represents the superhero Hercules is easily imagined as a warrior holding a massive club. The stars of Hercules aren't very bright, but the shapes they make are very noticeable. The top half of the body contains a four-star trapezoid shape, known as the Keystone asterism. Together with the "leg" stars, it forms a backward letter K at the center of the constellation. In Greek mythology, Hercules was the half-mortal son of Zeus. Zeus's wife and queen of the gods, Hera, didn't like Hercules and always looked for ways to harm him. Once, she made him lose his mind, causing him to kill his family. To repent, he took on 12 nearly impossible tasks, known as the Labors of Hercules. Displaying superhuman strength, Hercules completed the tasks and was made immortal.

SPOT THIS

ABOUT 21 STARS MAKE UP THE BIG FORM OF HERCULES (ABOVE). LOOK EAST OF THE BRIGHT STAR VEGA IN LYRA FOR THE BACKWARD K OF THE TORSO AND LEGS.

Did you know?

Over thousands of years, many cultures have recognized the human form in Hercules. For the seafaring Phoenicians in what is now the country of Lebanon, the constellation represented a local god. In ancient Iraq, the people saw it as the famous king Gilgamesh.

EXPERT'S CIRCLE

Hercules contains one of the best globular clusters in the northern sky—M13, located on the west side of the Keystone asterism. You can see it as a blur with the naked eye, a sharper image with binoculars, and a more detailed one with a three-inch (7.5-cm) telescope.

HYDRA THE SEA SERPENT

VITALS Hydra the Sea Serpent · **MAKEUP** 17 stars · **BEST VIEWED** March and April · **LOCATION** Spring, southwest quadrant · **ALPHA STAR** Alphard · **SIZE** 🖐️ 🖐️ 🖐️ ⯪

Hydra the Sea Serpent is the longest constellation, covering more area of the sky than any other. It used to be even bigger when it included three groupings of stars that are now separate constellations: Sextans, Corvus, and Crater. Hydra's kite-shaped head lies close to the constellation Cancer, while its tail drops down toward the southern horizon, near Libra. In Greek mythology, Hydra was the multiheaded sea serpent that the superhero Hercules was assigned to kill as one of his 12 labors. But the task was tricky, because each time Hercules chopped off a head, two grew back in its place. He finally stopped the regrowth by burning each stump. The constellation Hydra has only one head, and although the constellation covers a lot of area, its stars are pretty dim. The brightest star is Alphard, known as the "heart" of the serpent. Pick a dark spot on a clear spring night for the best Hydra viewing.

Did you know?

Ptolemy included Hydra in the list of 48 constellations he made in the second century. Later astronomers created separate constellations from some of Hydra's parts. But a plan to turn part of Hydra into a cat constellation never happened.

TO LOCATE HYDRA, LOOK FOR ITS HEART, ALPHARD (ABOVE). FIND ALPHARD JUST EAST OF A LINE FROM REGULUS IN LEO TO SIRIUS IN CANIS MAJOR.

be a SKYWATCHER!

LOOK FOR THIS! The spiral galaxy near the tail of Hydra known as the Southern Pinwheel (M83) is a good place to hunt for a supernova. You can spot the galaxy with binoculars, but you'll need a telescope to see any details.

LACERTA THE LIZARD

VITALS **Lacerta the Lizard** · MAKEUP **9 stars** · BEST VIEWED **March and April** · LOCATION **Spring, southwest quadrant** · ALPHA STAR **Alpha Lacertae** · SIZE (👆)

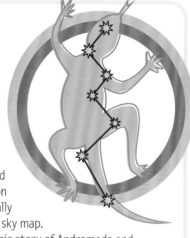

Like a sneaky lizard hiding in the grass, Lacerta is a faint collection of stars that the Polish astronomer Johannes Hevelius included in a star atlas published in the 17th century. Considered a small mammal at first, the constellation later morphed into a lizard. Hevelius finally used this shape to fill a small hole in the sky map.

Lacerta is now a tiny bystander to the epic story of Andromeda and Perseus that is taking place around it. Although Lacerta's stars are faint, they have a distinctive shape that zigzags between Cassiopeia, Cygnus, and Andromeda. The stars remain visible to observers of the northern sky for much of the year. They appear almost directly overhead in early fall for many skywatchers in North America.

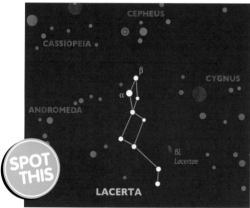

LOOK FOR LACERTA BELOW CASSIOPEIA. LIKE THAT QUEENLY CONSTELLATION, LACERTA HAS A W SHAPE (ART, AT TOP).

Did you know?

The deep-sky object BL Lacertae was first thought to be a variable star, but later it was found to be an elliptical galaxy with an active core.

EXPERT'S CIRCLE

Quasars—high-energy sky objects—give off radio signals that scientists think are the result of a black hole sucking in surrounding material. Blazars (left) are superstrong quasars that likely are the products of supermassive black holes. BL Lacertae is an example of a blazar.

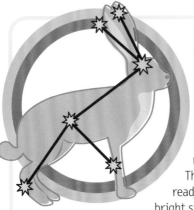

LEPUS THE HARE

VITALS Lepus the Hare ◦ **MAKEUP 13 stars** ◦ **BEST VIEWED January and February** ◦ **LOCATION Winter, southeast quadrant** ◦ **ALPHA STAR Arneb** ◦ **SIZE** ☝

Just as Orion keeps his hunting dogs close to him, he also has his prey nearby in the form of Lepus the Hare. This small constellation sits crouched and ready to hop away just west of Sirius, the bright star belonging to Canis Major, the Larger Dog. Not a great place to be if you're a hare! Midwinter marks Lepus's highest position in the sky, but the Hare remains close to the horizon for viewers in much of North America. It will dip below the horizon and out of sight for at least part of the year. Lepus contains the globular cluster M79, which may have been formed in the neighboring Canis Major dwarf galaxy. It's unusual to find a globular cluster in a southern constellation because most others are found at the center of the Milky Way, some 60,000 light-years away.

Did you know?

Before the Greeks decided to use the form of a hare for this constellation, this group of stars was seen as Orion's chair, or a boat used by the Egyptian god of the afterlife, Osiris.

IN MIDWINTER, LOOK FOR THE STARS REPRESENTING THE HARE'S EARS DIRECTLY BELOW RIGEL, THE LEFT FOOT OF THE CONSTELLATION ORION (ABOVE). HIND'S CRIMSON STAR IS RIGHT OF LEPORIS, WHICH IS LABELED WITH THE GREEK LETTER μ.

LOOK FOR THIS! With binoculars, try to spot Hind's Crimson star. This red variable star displays a wide range of brightness over the course of a bit more than a year, becoming redder as the brightness decreases.

LYNX THE LYNX

VITALS Lynx the Lynx · MAKEUP 8 stars · BEST VIEWED February and March · LOCATION Winter, northeast quadrant · ALPHA STAR Al Fahd SIZE

Hovering just above Gemini and below Ursa Major, Lynx is one of the modern constellations. It is also one of the harder ones to spot. The Polish astronomer Johannes Hevelius introduced it in the late 17th century to fill an empty spot on the sky map. He is said to have named it Lynx because you need the supersharp eyes of a cat to make out its dim stars. The shape of Lynx depicts the northern forest cat rearing up on its back legs, its feet planted in the sky near the constellation Leo and its head stretching out to Camelopardalis. Because this constellation came so late to the sky map, there are no entertaining tales from Greek mythology to explain it. But there are a number of double stars within it to reward the observer using even a small telescope.

TO VIEW LYNX, LOOK NORTH OF THE STARS CASTOR AND POLLUX IN THE CONSTELLATION GEMINI (ABOVE).

Laugh Out Loud!

Did you hear about the astronomy professor who didn't win the Nobel Prize?

A. He got a constellation prize instead!

be a SKYWATCHER!

LOOK FOR THIS! Near Lynx is a deep-sky object known as the Intergalactic Wanderer (NGC 2419), visible with a telescope (see largest circle at right). The astronomer Harlow Shapley gave it that name because the object is so far from the core of the Milky Way that it might break free of its loose orbit and leave our galaxy altogether some day!

LYRA THE LYRE

VITALS Lyra the Lyre • **MAKEUP** 6 stars • **BEST VIEWED** July and August • **LOCATION** Summer, center of chart • **ALPHA STAR** Vega • **SIZE** 🎵

Lyra is one of the jewels of the summer sky. It's a simple six-star pattern that looks like its namesake, the small harp known as a lyre. The constellation is centered around the superbright star Vega, part of the Summer Triangle asterism. The story behind Lyra is a sad one. The great god Apollo taught his son, Orpheus, to play the lyre. A lot of women admired Orpheus, but he loved only his wife, Eurydice. He loved her so much that when she died he followed her to the underworld and asked that she be allowed to return to him. The gods agreed, but only if Orpheus promised not to look at her as they left. He broke that promise, and when the gods took Eurydice back, Orpheus was so sad that he allowed himself to be killed. To honor this strong love, Zeus placed Orpheus's lyre in the sky.

Did you know?

The Ring Nebula, or M57 (right), is a softly glowing, doughnut-shaped gas cloud that appears between Lyra's two lower stars. The gas was the dying remnants of a star similar to our sun. You can view it with a small telescope.

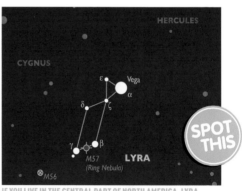

SPOT THIS

IF YOU LIVE IN THE CENTRAL PART OF NORTH AMERICA, LYRA (ABOVE) IS DIRECTLY OVERHEAD IN SUMMER.

EXPERT'S CIRCLE

Lights that are closer to us appear brighter, so how can we be sure one star really is brighter than the other? Scientists use a scale to compare stars based on how bright they appear (apparent magnitude) from Earth. Smaller numbers, especially negative ones, are brighter. Our sun (at left), for example, measures -26. On the same scale, Vega measures only 0.3. But if Vega and the sun were the same distance from Earth, Vega would be 58 times brighter than the sun. Vega's "built-in" brightness, or intrinsic magnitude, is a lot greater than the sun's (see also page 51).

MONOCEROS THE UNICORN

VITALS **Monoceros the Unicorn** ▪ MAKEUP **8 stars** ▪ BEST VIEWED **January and February** ▪ LOCATION **Winter, southeast quadrant** ▪ ALPHA STAR **Ctesias** ▪ SIZE 🖐

Monoceros the Unicorn was placed on sky maps in 1624 by German astronomer Jakob Bartsch. The constellation appears within the famous Winter Triangle asterism, composed of Betelgeuse in Orion, Procyon in Canis Minor, and Sirius in Canis Major. Monoceros is dim compared to those very bright stars, but it fills an important gap on the sky chart. Its position on the Milky Way provides it with some good objects for reference points. One object is the open star cluster M50, which appears between Procyon and Sirius and can be spotted through binoculars. Monoceros may represent a biblical creature that decided to play in the rain rather than join Noah and the other animals on the ark to escape the Great Flood.

DRAW A LINE FROM SIRIUS TO PROCYON TO BETELGEUSE AND YOU'LL FIND THE CENTER OF MONOCEROS IN THE MIDDLE (ABOVE).

Did you know?

Let's break down the name Monoceros. The "mono" part means "one." And "ceros" comes from the Greek word for "horn." Put them together and you get "one-horned"—which, of course, is what a unicorn is!

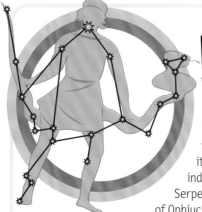

OPHIUCHUS THE SERPENT BEARER

VITALS Ophiuchus the Serpent Bearer ∘ MAKEUP 15 stars ∘ BEST VIEWED June and July ∘ LOCATION Summer, center of chart ∘ ALPHA STAR Rasalhague ∘ SIZE

The constellation Ophiuchus is only a fraction of the size it used to be. Once it included the stars that now form the independent constellation Serpens the Serpent, located in two parts on either side of Ophiuchus. Ophiuchus represents the god of medicine, Asclepius, who learned of the healing power of plants from a snake. Asclepius used this knowledge to cure the hunter Orion of a deadly scorpion bite—from Scorpius, of course. This made Hades, god of the underworld, jealous because he thought he'd lose his power to cause death. So Hades had Zeus kill Asclepius. Now the serpent bearer and serpent watch from the sky. The alpha star Rasalhague forms the head of Ophiuchus. The constellation is rich in deep-sky objects, including a bunch of globular clusters that are all visible with binoculars.

be a SKYWATCHER!

LOOK FOR THIS!
Ophiuchus is rich in star clusters marked as Messier numbers scattered throughout the constellation. All are visible with binoculars.

LOOK WEST OF THE MILKY WAY AND JUST ABOVE SCORPIUS TO LOCATE OPHIUCHUS (ABOVE). IT'S EASY TO IMAGINE THE SHAPE OF A BODY, LEGS, AND ARMS.

Did you know?

Stars appear still because they're so far away. But they do move! Over 180 years scientists measured the change in Barnard's star, in Ophiuchus. It is too faint to see. It moved 2,159 miles (3,475 km)—the same distance as the moon's diameter.

PERSEUS THE HERO

VITALS Perseus the Hero · **MAKEUP** 20 stars · **BEST VIEWED** November and December · **LOCATION** Autumn, northeast quadrant · **ALPHA STAR** Mirfak · **SIZE**

Perseus was a superhero of Greek mythology, and his awesome constellation really lives up to his reputation. He was a half-human son of Zeus and a big favorite among the gods, who gave him a powerful, shiny shield. Perseus used it like a mirror when he battled the monster Medusa. Seeing the reflection of her deadly gaze killed Medusa, and then Perseus cut off her head. Later, when rescuing Andromeda from the sea monster Cetus, Perseus used Medusa's head with its killer gaze to turn Cetus to stone. The constellation Perseus resembles a man and occurs in the part of the sky with others from the Perseus tale, such as Andromeda and Cassiopeia. It contains many bright and easily spotted stars and the excellent Perseid meteor shower in August. It also includes the double star clusters NGC 869 and NGC 884 that can be viewed through binoculars.

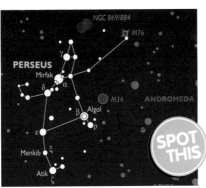

PERSEUS (ABOVE) STRADDLES THE MILKY WAY BETWEEN CASSIOPEIA AND ANDROMEDA.

NAME GAME

Over the centuries, the variable star Algol has been given a pretty creepy personality. Some people considered it the ghostly head of Medusa. Others saw it as the eye of a vampire. And the word "ghoul" comes from Algol, the Arabic name for the star, which means "demon's head."

be a SKYWATCHER!

LOOK FOR THIS! Look for the variable star Algol in Perseus. It dims on a three-day cycle, so if you get a few clear nights in a row you might be able to track its changes.

ERIDANUS THE RIVER

VITALS Eridanus the River · MAKEUP 33 stars · BEST VIEWED December and January · LOCATION Winter, southwest quadrant · ALPHA STAR Achernar · SIZE

The constellation Eridanus is a meandering river. It starts near Rigel, the left-foot star of Orion the Hunter, and winds its way south. It ends in the bright binary star Achernar (see page 58). Eridanus is so large that most people in the United States and Canada won't be able to see its southern end, including Achernar. It will be below the horizon for most locations. By tradition, Eridanus represents one of the great rivers of the ancient world. Some saw it as the Euphrates, the river that made possible the civilization of Mesopotamia in what is now the country of Iraq. Others saw it as the Nile, the river that provided fertile soil for the farmers of ancient Egypt. For the ancient Greeks, it was the river into which Phaethon, son of the sun god Helios, was cast after he failed to control Helios's chariot and Earth was in danger of burning up.

FIND RIGEL IN ORION TO LOCATE THE BEGINNING OF ERIDANUS AS IT FIRST TRAVELS WEST, AND THEN SOUTH. UNLESS YOU LIVE SOUTH OF MIAMI, FLORIDA, YOU WON'T BE ABLE TO SEE THE END STAR, ACHERNAR.

SPOT THIS

Laugh Out Loud!

Why didn't the college student do well in his astronomy class?

A. Because it was over his head!

In the past few years, hundreds of planets have been found in orbit around stars outside our solar system. These are called exoplanets—"outside" planets—and some are being studied to see if they support any kind of life. The star Epsilon Eridani, near the top of Eridanus, is orbited by exoplanets that scientists find interesting for their possibilities. You can view Epsilon Eridani (but not its exoplanets) with binoculars.

EXPERT'S CIRCLE

Spectacular Sky: Perseid Meteor Shower

Earthgrazer

Perseid meteors become more plentiful as the night of a shower progresses. But if you start your skywatching early, you might be lucky enough to see an "earthgrazer" (above), a meteor close to the horizon that will make a slow pass across your field of view. Earthgrazers are rare and would be seen as the constellation Perseus is rising and low in the sky.

Meteor showers occur in the evening and last long into the night. During the school year, especially in the middle of winter, it's hard to plan a meteor-watching party. But the Perseid shower—which occurs in the middle of August—arrives at the perfect time. For any meteor shower, check a website for the best viewing night, gather family and friends, pack a picnic and some lawn chairs, and head for a dark, open space. At their peak, the Perseids produce about 70 to 80 meteors per hour. The show is free and fantastic!

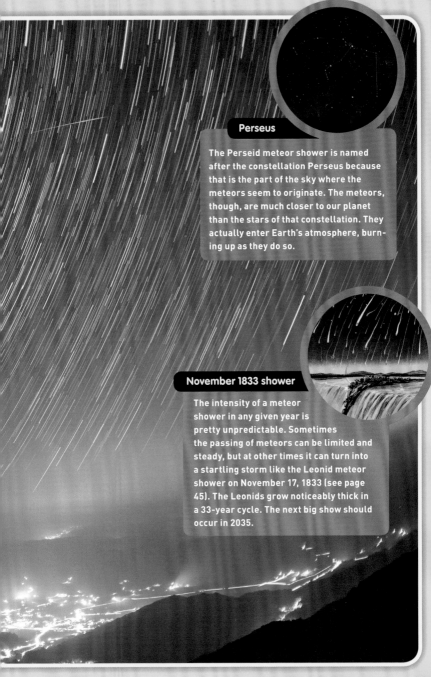

Perseus

The Perseid meteor shower is named after the constellation Perseus because that is the part of the sky where the meteors seem to originate. The meteors, though, are much closer to our planet than the stars of that constellation. They actually enter Earth's atmosphere, burning up as they do so.

November 1833 shower

The intensity of a meteor shower in any given year is pretty unpredictable. Sometimes the passing of meteors can be limited and steady, but at other times it can turn into a startling storm like the Leonid meteor shower on November 17, 1833 (see page 45). The Leonids grow noticeably thick in a 33-year cycle. The next big show should occur in 2035.

PISCIS AUSTRINUS THE SOUTHERN FISH

VITALS Piscis Austrinus the Southern Fish · **MAKEUP** 9 stars · **BEST VIEWED** September and October · **LOCATION** Autumn, southwest quadrant · **ALPHA STAR** Fomalhaut · **SIZE**

One of the original 48 constellations that the Greek astronomer Ptolemy identified in the second century, Piscis Austrinus is located in the "watery" section of the sky with other water-related constellations. Its main stars form a kind of fish or even whale shape that a preschooler might draw. In Greek mythology, the Southern Fish was considered to be a parent of the two fish in the constellation Pisces. It also was seen as a fish drinking water from the jug of nearby Aquarius. The ancient Assyrians saw it as a shape-shifting teacher, Oannes, who transformed into a fish at night. The constellation's alpha star, Fomalhaut, helps locate Piscis Austrinus, which lies low to the horizon even at its highest position during the year. Fomalhaut is regarded as a "young" star because it's only between 100 and 300 million years old! It ranks as the 18th brightest star to the naked eye and it seems even brighter because it appears in a dim section of the sky. Fomalhaut, which means "mouth of the fish," lies a mere 25 light-years from Earth.

SPOT THIS

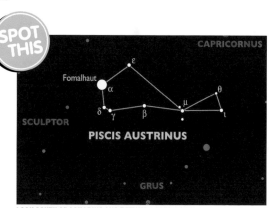

LOOK SOUTH OF AQUARIUS AND BETWEEN CAPRICORNUS AND GRUS TO FIND PISCIS AUSTRINUS (ABOVE).

Did you know?

In 2008, scientists using the Hubble Space Telescope took photos of a planet orbiting Fomalhaut. It was the first extrasolar planet, or exoplanet (a planet outside of our solar system), confirmed by direct observations—with pictures to prove it!

PUPPIS THE STERN

VITALS **Puppis the Stern** ▪ MAKEUP **12 stars** ▪ BEST VIEWED **February and March** ▪ LOCATION **Winter, southeast quadrant** ▪ ALPHA STAR **None (brightest: Zeta Puppis)** ▪ SIZE 🖐

You might think from its name that the constellation Puppis represents a cute little dog romping in the sky. But you would be wrong. Puppis is the stern, or back end, of a giant ship constellation known as Argo Navis that was divided into three constellations more than 250 years ago. The *Argo* is the ship that carried Jason and the Argonauts on the quest to steal the Golden Fleece from a nasty dragon. Puppis is shaped like a ship's rudder, the part that steers the ship. It occurs with the other pieces of the original constellation in the "watery" part of the night sky. Puppis lies in the rich starfields of the Milky Way and contains the M93 star cluster, visible through a telescope. When Puppis was created, the stars it received were not relabeled, so Puppis has no alpha star.

PUPPIS CAN BE SEEN LOW ON THE SOUTHERN HORIZON. LOCATE IT (ABOVE) BY TRACING A LINE FROM SIRIUS THE DOG STAR THROUGH THE STAR ADHARA, BOTH IN CANIS MAJOR (SEE PAGE 113).

SPOT THIS

Did you know?

Even though the constellation Puppis has no alpha star, it has a very bright zeta (ζ) star. Zeta Puppis is a blue supergiant that can be seen with the naked eye.

TRY THIS!

Star clusters may look like hazy blurs when viewed with the naked eye, but they come into focus with binoculars. To see this another way, use a paper punch to make holes in a sheet of white paper. Then glue the small circles close together on a piece of black paper. Look at the paper up close, then tape it to a wall. Walk away and look back. Notice the change?

SAGITTA THE ARROW

VITALS Sagitta the Arrow · **MAKEUP 6 stars**
· **BEST VIEWED August and September** · **LOCATION Summer chart,
southeast quadrant** · **ALPHA STAR Sham** · **SIZE** 👍

You don't have to work your imagination too hard to see an arrow in the
shape made by the main stars of the
constellation Sagitta. The third smallest
constellation, Sagitta lies totally within the
Summer Triangle asterism formed of Altair in
Aquila, Deneb in Cygnus, and Vega in Lyra. Most
ancient cultures associated these stars with an arrow, and there are a
number of arrow stories to choose from to explain Sagitta's presence
in the sky. In the myths of the Greeks and Romans, it could be the arrow
that Cupid (Eros) used to spread love, or the arrow Apollo used to slay
the Cyclops, or the one Hercules deployed to slay some nasty birds in
one of his 12 labors. Despite similar names, Sagitta and the constellation Sagittarius do not seem to be connected in sky mythology.

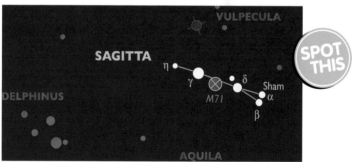

YOU'LL FIND SAGITTA (ABOVE) BETWEEN VULPECULA, AQUILA, AND DELPHINUS.

be a SKYWATCHER!

LOOK FOR THIS! The shaft of Sagitta's arrow
contains the deep-sky object M71. It's a globular
cluster that can be spotted with binoculars,
although a telescope will show the stars more
clearly. M71 is about 10 billion years old and
resides some 13,000 light-years from Earth!

SCUTUM THE SHIELD

VITALS **Scutum the Shield** · MAKEUP **5 stars** · BEST VIEWED **July and August** · LOCATION **Summer chart, southwest quadrant** · ALPHA STAR **Alpha Scuti** · SIZE

Ptolemy may have been the father of the constellations, but Johannes Hevelius probably put more of his personality into them—like a little brother or sister who gets to choose the name of the family pet. Scutum is one of the constellations named for an object, a very specific shield known as the Shield of Sobieski. John Sobieski was a king of Poland in the 17th century. He commanded an army of 70,000 soldiers that defeated the troops of the Ottoman Empire in a battle in Vienna, Austria, in 1683. The battle was particularly important because it stopped the Ottoman Turks from expanding their rule in Europe. To Hevelius, that seemed worthy of a constellation. But he had another reason to favor King John Sobieski and his shield. The king was Hevelius's patron, who gave him money so he could do his astronomy research.

YOU CAN FIND SCUTUM (ABOVE), ONE OF THE DIMMER CONSTELLATIONS, IN THE MILKY WAY BETWEEN SAGITTARIUS AND AQUILA.

Did you know?

The Chandra X-Ray Observatory has found many deep-space objects because of its ability to track and see parts of the electromagnetic spectrum invisible to the eye. Among its finds: a massive supernova (called G21.5-0.9) in Scutum involving a star ten times larger than the sun.

be a SKYWATCHER!

LOOK FOR THIS! The Wild Duck cluster (right), also known as M11 (above), is one of the Milky Way's densest star clusters, named to conjure the idea of a big flock of—you guessed it—ducks. You can see it with binoculars, to the southwest of Scutum's northern tip.

SEXTANS THE SEXTANT

VITALS Sextans the Sextant · **MAKEUP** 4 stars · **BEST VIEWED** March and April · **LOCATION** Spring, southwest quadrant · **ALPHA STAR** Alpha Sextantis · **SIZE** 🖐️

Not all constellations have interesting stories that describe the adventures of Greek gods and goddesses. Some constellations were just made up for places where there were gaps in the star chart. Most of the newer constellations have not been given human or animal shapes, and many are objects used in science. Sextans is one of these newer constellations. The stars in Sextans used to be thought of as the fin on the multiheaded monster constellation Hydra. But in the 17th century, Polish astronomer Johannes Hevelius separated them out as a constellation named for an instrument that is used to measure the position of stars: the sextant. Hevelius had recently lost a lot of his instruments in a fire, so maybe he was creating a memorial for his lost sextant. The stars that make up Sextans are not very bright, but they can be found in the space between the constellations Hydra and Leo.

Did you know?

Ancient Chinese astronomers often thought of stars as representing government officials. They named one of the stars in Sextans the "Minister of State in Heaven."

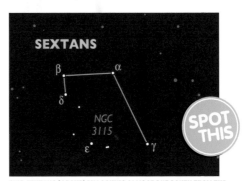

SEXTANS

β   α
δ

NGC
3115

ε   γ

SPOT THIS

FIND SEXTANS (ABOVE) BY LOOKING ALMOST DUE SOUTH FROM THE BRIGHT STAR REGULUS IN LEO. SEE THE SPINDLE GALAXY (NGC 3115) AT CHANDRA.HARVARD.EDU/PHOTO/2011/N3115/ZOOM.HTML.

EXPERT'S CIRCLE

There are different types of sextants. Sailors use mainly small, handheld sextants to measure the angle between stars and other objects and the horizon to help them navigate. Early astronomers (left) like Hevelius used larger astronomical sextants—several yards (meters) wide—to precisely measure the positions of stars in the sky.

TRIANGULUM THE TRIANGLE

VITALS Triangulum the Triangle • **MAKEUP** 3 stars • **BEST VIEWED** November and December • **LOCATION** Autumn, center of chart • **ALPHA STAR** Mothallah • **SIZE** (⌒)

The second-century Greek astronomer Ptolemy included the constellation now known as Triangulum on his original list of 48 constellations. This basic geometric pattern of three stars has had pretty much the same identity for thousands of years. The ancient Hebrews seem to have named it for the small percussion instrument—the triangle of metal that creates a ringing sound when struck. The Greeks sometimes called it Deltoton because it reminded them of their Greek letter delta (Δ). Some ancient writers connected the constellation to the Nile Delta, the fertile outlet of the long African river, or to the Italian island of Sicily. This theme continues in the name of Triangulum's alpha star, Mothallah, which means "triangle" in Arabic. This constellation is best seen from the Northern Hemisphere in December, when it is high and central in the sky.

LOOK FOR A FAINT BUT DISTINCT TRIANGLE BETWEEN ANDROMEDA, PERSEUS, AND ARIES.

Did you know?

The Pinwheel galaxy (M33) contains a black hole that is almost 16 times as massive as the sun. The black hole orbits a companion star that someday will likely turn into a supernova.

be a SKYWATCHER!

LOOK FOR THIS! The Pinwheel galaxy (M33) lies within the area of the constellation Triangulum. You can see it as a faint glow under clear conditions, but a telescope will reveal its pinwheel shape.

VITALS Ursa Major the Great Bear • **MAKEUP** 20 stars • **BEST VIEWED** March and April • **LOCATION** Spring, center of chart • **ALPHA STAR** Dubhe • **SIZE** 🖐️🖐️

Ursa Major is visible most of the year in the northern sky, giving the chance to really get to know this important constellation. It's a great bear in every way you can imagine. Twenty stars make up the bear's head and body. Its size spans two extended hands against the sky. It is large enough to contain the famous asterism, or star pattern, known as the Big Dipper. And the dipper itself contains the apparent binary stars Mizar and Alcor. The constellation is also home to the M81 and M101 galaxies, and to M97, known as the Owl Nebula. In Greek mythology, the Great Bear was a nymph, or fairy, named Callisto that the god Zeus paid a lot of attention to, making his wife, Hera, jealous. Hera changed Callisto into a bear. Then Callisto was nearly killed by the bear's hunter son, Arcas. To protect mother and son, Zeus placed them both in the sky.

USE THE SEVEN STARS OF THE BIG DIPPER (ABOVE) TO GET YOUR "BEARINGS" TO BUILD THE REST OF URSA MAJOR, VISIBLE OVERHEAD IN THE SPRING.

EXPERT'S CIRCLE

The stars Mizar and Alcor look like a binary pair, but it's a trick caused by the way they're lined up. They're way too far apart to be bound together by gravity.

be a SKYWATCHER!

LOOK FOR THIS! The M81 galaxy (above) is visible with binoculars, just above the outer edge of the Big Dipper's bowl.

URSA MINOR THE LITTLE BEAR

VITALS Ursa Minor the Little Bear ◦ **MAKEUP** 7 stars
◦ **BEST VIEWED** Year-round ◦ **LOCATION** On all charts, in the north
◦ **ALPHA STAR** Polaris ◦ **SIZE** 🖐

It may be called the Little Bear, but Ursa Minor is as important as its nearby "mother," Ursa Major. Ursa Minor is visible all year and contains Polaris, or the North Star, as its alpha star. For thousands of years, travelers, navigators, and skywatchers have found their way by locating the constant presence of Ursa Minor and Polaris, which represents the celestial North Pole. The Little Bear takes the form of a dipper, giving it the nickname Little Dipper and making it both a constellation and an asterism. In Greek myth it is Arcas, the child of Callisto, who is the target of Hera's jealous revenge. To protect them, Hera's husband, Zeus, placed the Little Bear and his mother close to each other in the sky. Polaris won't always be the North Star. The celestial pole shifts over the centuries, and after 2100, it will begin to move away from Polaris and begin a shift toward Vega, a transfer that will take about 12,000 years.

SPOT THIS

USE THE LINE FORMED BY THE OUTER EDGE OF THE BIG DIPPER TO LOCATE POLARIS IN THE HANDLE OF THE LITTLE DIPPER (ABOVE), AND YOU'VE FOUND URSA MINOR.

be a SKYWATCHER!

LOOK FOR THIS! During the third week of December, ask if you can stay up late one night to watch the Ursid meteor shower, coming from the area of Ursa Minor.

Did you know?

Polaris can reveal more than the direction north. Its distance above the horizon indicates latitude, or position on the Earth's surface north (or south) of the Equator. At the North Pole, Polaris is directly overhead. At the Equator, it is on the horizon. Can you predict where it will be in the sky based on where you live?

VULPECULA THE FOX

VITALS Vulpecula the Fox · **MAKEUP** 3 stars · **BEST VIEWED** August and September · **LOCATION** Summer, center of chart · **ALPHA STAR** Alpha Vulpeculae · **SIZE**

Polish astronomer Johannes Hevelius invented the constellation Vulpecula in the 17th century and originally named it Vulpecula cum ansere, Latin for "the fox with the goose." The goose part has dropped out of the name, but you can still find older drawings of the constellation that show a fox running along with a struggling goose in its jaws. The Fox is found high in the late summer sky, inside the band of the Milky Way. It's not an easy constellation to spot because it is far dimmer than its surroundings.

Did you know?

The constellation Vulpecula boasts several "firsts." It contains the Dumbell Nebula (M27), the first reported planetary nebula, and also the first radio pulsar (PSR B1919+21), a rotating star that emits intense radio signals.

SEARCH FOR THREE DIM STARS IN THE BRIGHT REGION OF THE MILKY WAY BETWEEN THE CONSTELLATIONS LYRA AND SAGITTA (ABOVE).

be a SKYWATCHER!

LOOK FOR THIS! You will probably need binoculars to find it, but between Vulpecula and Sagitta look for the Coathanger asterism, a group of ten stars—six form the bar and four form the hook—that looks remarkably like ... a coat hanger. Blue stars are superhot. White-yellow stars are less hot. Red stars are cool.

Find Out More

Want to find out even more about the night sky and everything in it? Check out these books, apps, websites, and videos. Be sure to ask an adult to help you search the Web to find the sites below.

BOOKS

Aldrin, Buzz. *Welcome to Mars: Making a Home on the Red Planet.* National Geographic, 2015.

National Geographic Kids Everything Space, 2015.

National Geographic Kids Space Encyclopedia, 2013.

APPS

Sky Orb, Star Chart, and Planets are all free astronomy apps for iPhone and Android systems.

WEBSITES

aas.org/education/EducatorResources — The American Astronomical Society has an array of resources for K-12.

astronomy.com — The website of *Astronomy* magazine offers news, photos, and other information, both articles and daily sky guides.

astro-observer.com/observing/software .html — This website has a collection of online tools and sky charts as well as links to many other resources.

constellationsofwords.com/Constellations/ Cetus.html — Provides more detailed information and drawings of the constellations.

Earthsky.org — This online magazine has general information and sky charts.

hubblesite.org — NASA's website for all images from the Hubble Space Telescope features photo galleries, videos, blogs, technology, discoveries, and daily updates.

janus.astro.umd.edu/ — The tools and animations on this site help visualize the solar system, night sky, and other aspects of astronomy.

nasa.gov/mission_pages/newhorizons/ main/index.html — NASA's website for the New Horizons Pluto Flyby features the latest photographs, videos, discoveries, and more.

nasa.gov/missions — Features an alphabetic guide to NASA missions.

skyandtelescope.com — The website of *Sky and Telescope* magazine also has interactive guides, charts, and other information.

swpc.noaa.gov — The website for the NOAA Space Weather Prediction Center has information about solar storms and sunspots, as well as meteor showers and auroras.

VIDEOS

Institute of Physics — iop.org/resources/ videos/education/classroom/astronomy/ page_51897.html — The institute offers a collection of videos and other resources for teachers.

National Geographic Journey to the Edge of the Universe

National Geographic Ultimate Space: Into the Cosmos

SOLAR AND LUNAR ECLIPSES: 2017 and 2018

Each year you'll have a chance to see both lunar and solar eclipses. Check out the times and types below.

There are three kinds of lunar eclipses: partial (when part of Earth's shadow falls on the moon); total (when all of Earth's shadow covers it); and penumbral (when Earth's outer shadow slightly darkens the moon's surface but doesn't fully cover it).

Solar eclipses include these three types: total (when Earth's shadow covers the sun); partial (when the moon passes in front of the sun but doesn't completely cover it); and annular (when the sun looks like a ring of fire behind the moon's shadow).

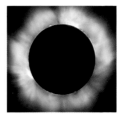

Partial Solar Eclipse   Partial Lunar Eclipse   Annular Solar Eclipse

Date	Solar/Lunar	Eclipse type	Where you can see it
February 11, 2017	Lunar	Penumbral	Americas, Europe, Africa, Asia
February 26, 2017	Solar	Annular	South America, Africa, Antarctica
August 7, 2017	Lunar	Partial	Europe, Africa, Asia, Australia
August 21, 2017	Solar	Total	North Pacific, United States, South Atlantic
January 31, 2018	Lunar	Total	Asia, Australia, Pacific, western North America
February 15, 2018	Solar	Partial	Antarctica, southern South America
July 13, 2018	Solar	Partial	Southern Australia
July 27, 2018	Lunar	Total	South America, Europe, Africa, Asia, Australia
August 11, 2018	Solar	Partial	Northern Europe, northeast Asia

ANNUAL METEOR SHOWERS AND THEIR DATES

It's worth it to stay up late to see a meteor shower! The showers below happen about the same time each year, but for annual predictions, see amsmeteors.org/meteor-showers/meteor-shower-calendar. For best viewing, follow these tips: (1) Find a dark, open sky away from city lights. (2) Know the dates and times for the current year. (3) Settle in with a blanket, a lawn chair, a hot drink, and binoculars.

Shower	Constellation where it originates	Dates	When it's most visible
Quadrantids	Draco	January 1–5	January 3
Lyrids	Lyra	April 16–25	April 21
Eta Aquarids	Aquarius	April 19–May 28	May 4
Delta Aquarids	Aquarius	July 21–August 23	July 28
Perseids	Perseus	July 17–August 24	August 12
Orionids	Orion	Sept. 10–Oct. 26	October 22
Leonids	Leo	November 14–21	November 17
Geminids	Gemini	December 7–17	December 13

Glossary

APOGEE: The farthest point an orbiting celestial body reaches in relation to the object it is orbiting around

ASTERISM: A distinct shape formed by a group of stars that has not been accepted as a constellation

ASTEROID: A rock floating in the solar system that is not large enough to be a dwarf planet

ASTEROID BELT: Area between Mars and Jupiter that is filled with asteroids

ASTRONOMICAL UNIT: The distance from the sun to Earth, or about 93 million miles (150 million km)

ATMOSPHERE: The layer of gases attached to a planet by gravity. It helps create weather patterns and, in Earth's case, provides protection from stellar radiation

AURORA (BOREALIS AND AUSTRALIS): Lights in the sky caused by the interaction of the solar wind with Earth's atmosphere

BINARY STAR: A pair of stars that are locked together by gravity

BLACK HOLE: A mysterious dead star so dense its gravity does not allow even light to escape

BLAZAR: A strong quasar

CEPHEID: A type of variable star that changes from bright to dim in a regular cycle that can last a few days or a few months

COMET: A small body composed of ice and dust that orbits the sun on an oval path. When it's near the sun, the comet nucleus heats up and lets off jets of gas and long tails of gas and dust.

CONJUNCTION: The apparently close approach of one celestial body to another. This refers to two planets that look to be near each other or the moon.

CONSTELLATIONS: Groups of stars that create a distinct shape and often have a story. Some were named by the ancient Greek astronomer Ptolemy. Others were later recognized by the International Astronomical Union.

DEGREE: A unit of measurement that refers to either temperature or a geometric angle. Your forefinger held at arm's length is about two degrees wide.

DWARF PLANET: A member of the solar system that is larger than an asteroid but does not qualify as a planet

EARTH'S ROTATION: The motion Earth makes as it turns on its axis. One complete turn takes 24 hours and marks the beginning and end of one Earth day.

ECLIPSE: When one celestial body passes in front of another and blocks it from view to observers on the Earth

ECLIPTIC: The imaginary line that the sun travels through the constellations during an entire year

EQUATOR: The imaginary line that runs around the middle of Earth or sky chart

EQUINOX: The two days when the amount of daylight and darkness are almost equal, marking the change of the season from winter to spring and summer to fall

EXOPLANET: Also called an extrasolar planet; a planet circling a star other than the sun

EYEPIECE: The part of a telescope or binocular that a user looks through

GALAXY: A massive collection of stars held together by gravity

GAS GIANTS: The large, gaseous planets beyond Mars, including Jupiter, Saturn, Uranus, and Neptune

GPS: Global positioning system, or the network of satellites that allows computers, phones, and other devices to determine location on land or at sea

GRAVITY: The pull that every object in the universe exerts on every other object; gravity increases with an object's mass

GREEN FLASH: A rare green spot on the horizon caused as the atmosphere filters different colors from the light of the setting sun

KUIPER BELT: An area between Neptune and Pluto in which dwarf planets orbit the sun

LENS: The part of a telescope or binocular that collects light and makes objects appear larger

LIGHT-YEAR: The distance light travels in a year

M-OBJECTS (LIKE M52): The numbers assigned by French astronomer Charles Messier to objects as he identified them. See also *Messier Catalog*.

MAGNETIC FIELD: An area of magnetic force around a source of magnetism, like the sun, a planet, or other sky object

MAGNITUDE: The brightness of a star, either as it appears (apparent magnitude) or as it would appear from a fixed distance (intrinsic magnitude)

MESSIER CATALOG: The list of objects including nebulae, galaxies, and star clusters Charles Messier made to keep track of objects in the sky

METEOR: Sometimes called a shooting star; a bit of space debris that brightly burns up as it enters Earth's atmosphere

MILKY WAY: Earth's home galaxy

MIRA VARIABLE: A type of old reddish star that pulsates regularly, changing brightness by many magnitudes over a period of 100 days or longer

NEBULA: A massive gas cloud where stars are born. Plural: nebulae

NOVA: A white dwarf star that brightens suddenly as it pulls gas away from a companion star and the gas explodes. Plural: novae

NUCLEAR FUSION: A reaction that powers the sun and stars by giving off light, heat, and other forms of energy. It occurs when atoms of elements like hydrogen are packed together under intense pressure.

OORT CLOUD: An area of orbiting chunks of ice at the outer edge of the solar system. The chunks sometimes break free and become comets.

ORBIT: The path that one celestial body follows around a larger body. Gravity from the larger body keeps the orbiting body from floating away.

PERIGEE: The closest point an orbiting celestial body comes to the object it is orbiting around

PERIOD: The time it takes for a variable star to change from bright to dim and back again

PLANET: A body in space that fulfills three rules set by the International Astronomical Union: (1) It must orbit a star. (2) It must be big enough for gravity to squash it into a sphere. (3) It must be big enough to clear its path of floating debris: Often, that means sweeping up the smaller objects in its orbit.

Glossary

POLE: The point at the end of a planet's imaginary axis that marks its extreme north (top) or south (bottom)

PRECESSION: A slow wobble in Earth's rotation axis caused by the gravitational pull of the sun and other planets. One precession cycle for Earth lasts about 26,000 years.

PULSAR: A rapidly spinning neutron star that flashes periodic bursts of radio (and sometimes visible) energy

QUADRANT: In a galaxy, it's the system that divides space into four quarters. In the Milky Way, the sun is at the imaginary center.

QUASAR: Thought to be the active core of a very distant and very bright galaxy, possibly powered by a supermassive black hole

RED GIANT: A reddish or orange star (such as Betelgeuse in Orion) in a late stage of its evolution. It is relatively cool and has expanded its outer shell of gas to perhaps 100 times its original size.

SOLAR FLARE: Eruption of trapped energy from the surface of the sun

SOLAR SYSTEM: The sun, its surrounding planets, and all of the asteroids and dwarf planets the sun holds in its orbit

SOLSTICE: The day of most and least sunlight, marking the change of season from spring to summer and fall to winter

SPEED OF LIGHT: 186,000 miles a second (300,000 km/s)

SPIRAL GALAXY: A galaxy with a distinct spiral shape, with arms radiating from the center. The Milky Way is a spiral galaxy.

STAR: A ball of gas with enough internal pressure to start nuclear fusion. Our sun is a star.

SUNDIAL: The earliest instrument for telling time. A sundial has a fixed set of markers. As the sun moves over the markers, it casts shadows that tell the time of day or year.

SUPERNOVA: The explosion of a massive star in which it blows off its outer layers of atmosphere. It may be as bright as an entire galaxy for a while.

TERRESTRIAL PLANETS: The dense, rocky planets closest to the sun, including Mercury, Venus, Earth, and Mars

TIDES: The daily rise and fall in Earth's oceans, seas, and rivers caused by the gravitational tug of the moon and to a lesser extent the sun

TRANSIT: When one celestial body crosses the face of another from the perspective of an observer on Earth

VARIABLE STAR: A star whose brightness changes over time

WHITE DWARF: The small, hot remnant left when a red giant star loses its outer layers

ZODIAC: A collection of 12 constellations known as "the circle of animals" that travel the ecliptic through the year and are associated with the pseudoscience of astrology

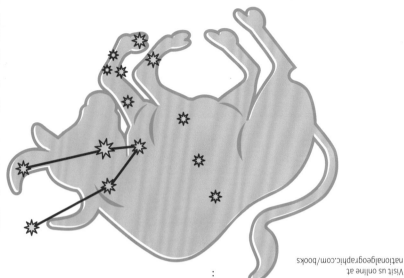

National Geographic Partners, LLC, and Potomac Global Media, LLC, would like to thank the following members of the project team: Kevin Mulroy, Barbara Brownell Grogan, Howard Schneider, Catherine Herbert Howell, Christopher L. Mazzatenta, Matt Propert, Robert Burnham, Jane Sunderland, and Tim Griffin.

Since 1888, the National Geographic Society has funded more than 12,000 research, exploration, and preservation projects around the world. The Society receives funds from National Geographic Partners LLC, funded in part by your purchase. A portion of the proceeds from this book supports this vital work. To learn more, visit www.natgeo.com/info.

For more information, visit nationalgeographic.com, call 1-877-873-6846, or write to the following address:

National Geographic Partners
1145 17th Street N.W.
Washington, D.C. 20036-4688 U.S.A.

Visit us online at
nationalgeographic.com/books

For librarians and teachers:
ngchildrensbooks.org

More for kids from National Geographic:
natgeokids.com

For information about special discounts for bulk purchases, please contact National Geographic Books Special Sales: specialsales@natgeo.com

For rights or permissions inquiries, please contact National Geographic Books Subsidiary Rights: bookrights@natgeo.com

NATIONAL GEOGRAPHIC and Yellow Border Design are trademarks of the National Geographic Society, used under license.

Editorial, Design, and Production by Potomac Global Media, LLC

Art Directed by Jim Hiscott, Jr.
Designed by Christopher L. Mazzatenta

Paperback ISBN: 978-1-4263-2546-5

Reinforced library binding ISBN:
978-1-4263-2547-2

Printed in China
19/RRDH/4 (paperback)
19/RRDH/2 (RLB)